Fodor's
25 Best

ROME

Contents

KEY TO SYMBOLS

➕ Map reference to the accompanying pull-out map

✉ Address

☎ Telephone number

🕐 Opening/closing times

🍴 Restaurant or café

🚆 Nearest rail station

Ⓜ Nearest Metro (subway) station

🚌 Nearest bus route

ENTERTAINMENT 128

Whether you're after a cultural fix or just want a place to relax with a drink after a hard day's sightseeing, we've made the best choices for you.

EAT 138

Uncover great dining experiences, from a quick bite at lunch to top-notch evening meals.

SLEEP 152

We've brought together the best hotels in the city, whatever budget you're on.

NEED TO KNOW 160

The practical information you need to make your trip run smoothly.

PULL-OUT MAP

The pull-out map with this book is a comprehensive street plan of the city. We've given grid references within the book for each sight and listing.

🚢 Nearest riverboat or ferry stop
♿ Facilities for visitors with disabilities
🛈 Tourist information
❓ Other practical information

💷 Admission charges: Expensive (over €15), Moderate (€9–€15) and Inexpensive (under €9)
▷ Further information

Introducing Rome

Rome is one of the world's great cities, the city of the Caesars, of romance and *la dolce vita*, of long, hot, sunny days, of superb art galleries, churches and museums, of fountain-splashed piazzas and majestic monuments to its golden age of empire.

Rome is a city with all the myriad pleasures of any Italian destination—notably superb food and wine—as well as great bars, cafés and shopping, vibrant nightlife and numerous cultural events. At the same time, Rome is very much a contemporary city—traffic rumbles around medieval cobbled streets—though the skyline bristles not with glittering skyscrapers but with the domes of churches and palaces.

But how to visit a city where there is so much to see? First of all don't rush to the Colosseum, St. Peter's or the Sistine Chapel on your first morning. Rome for much of the year is hot and crowded. If you try to cram in too much, or soldier on through the heat, the chances are you'll emerge battered rather than enraptured. Instead, stroll around the Ghetto or Trastevere, two of the city's quaintest old quarters, or have a cappuccino in one of Rome's loveliest squares, Campo de' Fiori or Piazza Navona. Or head for one of the lesser-known art-filled churches, such as San Luigi dei Francesi or Santa Maria del Popolo, crammed with masterpieces by Raphael, Pinturicchio and Caravaggio.

Once gently acclimatized, and hopefully charmed by the city's quieter side, you can begin to think about the Trevi Fountain, the Spanish Steps, the Roman Forum or the Vatican Museums. And don't forget some of the relatively unsung museums—notably the Palazzo Altemps and Palazzo Massimo alle Terme, both devoted to Classical art and sculpture, or the MAXXI gallery, an architectural *tour de force* that is given over to contemporary art.

Bear in mind this is a living city with more than 3,000 years of history. One, two, even ten visits aren't enough to do it justice. However much you see, one thing is for certain, you'll be back.

FACTS AND FIGURES

- Population estimate in 2019: 2,872,800.
- The official age of Rome in 2019 is 2,772 years.
- There have been 266 popes and 73 emperors.
- The city covers an area of 1,494sq km (577sq miles).
- Vatican City covers an area of 0.44sq km (0.17sq miles) and is the world's smallest state.

SECRET KEYHOLE

Rome's most charming view is from Piazza dei Cavalieri di Malta on the Aventine Hill. To find it, walk to the left of the church of Santa Sabina and to the end of the piazza; look through the keyhole of the door (No. 3) of the Priory of the Knights of Malta. Through this tiny hole you will see a secret garden and an avenue of trees framing… But let's not spoil the surprise: see for yourself.

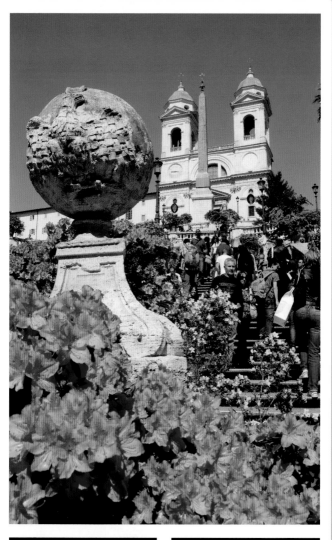

WATERY WASTE

More than 50 of Rome's fountains are fed by the waters of the Aqua Virgo, a source that the Romans brought into the city in 19BC. It flows from the countryside outside the city, and feeds the Barcaccia fountain at the foot of the Spanish Steps, before supplying many others, including the most famous of them all, the delightful Trevi Fountain.

SWISS GUARD

The pope's official bodyguards are recruited from Switzerland's four predominantly Catholic cantons. Each guard must be between 19 and 25, at least 1.75m (5ft 9in) tall and remain unmarried during their tour of duty. Their distinctive uniforms, which may have been designed by Michelangelo, are in the hues of the Medici popes—red, yellow and blue.

Focus On Bernini

Many have changed the face of Rome over the centuries—artists, emperors, tyrants and popes—but few have had a more lasting or more widespread effect on the very fabric of the city than Gian Lorenzo Bernini, a sculptor and architect whose piazzas, sculptures, follies and fountains you will encounter time and again in the Eternal City.

Papal Favor

Bernini was born in Naples in 1598, the son of Angelica Galante and Pietro Bernini, a Florentine sculptor. By the age of seven he was accompanying his father to Rome and assisting him in artistic commissions, work that eventually brought him to the attention of Pope Paul V and the Pope's affluent nephew, Cardinal Scipione Borghese. The patronage of the papacy and of wealthy Roman families such as the Borghese was essential for any artist hoping to work and succeed in Rome, especially during the baroque era, when the city's churches, palaces and public spaces were undergoing a dramatic transformation.

Bernini's output would be prodigious, and he would go on to work under several popes, combining undoubted talent with a shrewd awareness of how to play his wealthy patrons. In this he was in distinct contrast to his rival of the period, Francesco Borromini, a more inventive architect, but a troubled soul whose dark disposition won him few friends and fewer commissions.

St. Peter's

Bernini's mark on Rome is most apparent in its principal religious building, St. Peter's (▷ 14–15), where he designed the great piazza in front of the church, parts of the facade and much of the interior, including the colossal *baldacchino,* or canopy, above the altar. He also designed the church of Sant'Andrea al

Clockwise from top left: The Rape of Proserpina, Museo e Galleria Borghese; Fontana del Nettuno, Piazza Navona; Apollo and Daphne, Museo e Galleria

Quirinale and had a hand in several palaces, notably the Palazzo Barberini (▷ 36–37), Palazzo Montecitorio and Palazzo Chigi-Odaleschi. When you stop to admire a fountain in Rome, the chances are that it will be the work of Bernini, from the most prominent—the Fontana dei Quattro Fiumi in Piazza Navona (▷ 46–47)—to more idiosyncratic fancies such as the Barcaccia fountain (▷ 48–49) at the foot of the Spanish Steps, and the Fontana delle Api and Fontana del Tritone (▷ 68) in Piazza Barberini.

Masterpieces

Bernini's consummate architectural skill was in creating public spaces, as in the Piazza San Pietro, or adapting existing churches and palaces in ways that were sympathetic to their surroundings. His sculptural skills—and he was the foremost sculptor of his day and the greatest since Michelangelo—were a peerless technique and the ability to capture a narrative moment in stone.

Both dramatic and dynamic qualities can be seen best in his masterpieces in the Galleria Borghese (▷ 30–31), housed in the sumptuous palace of his old patron, Cardinal Scipione Borghese. Here is David caught in the act of casting his sling at Goliath; Daphne turning into a laurel tree to escape the clutches of Apollo; and the abductor's hand sinking into the soft thigh of his victim in *The Rape of Proserpina*. These are dazzling, virtuoso works, intended to impress, but Bernini can also be witty and quiet, and it is his smaller works you'll find dotted around Rome that you may well remember best after you leave the city: the charming turtles added to the Fontana delle Tartarughe (▷ 68), for example, or his "Breezy Angels" on the Ponte Sant'Angelo and the quaint little elephant and obelisk in front of Santa Maria sopra Minerva (▷ 54–55).

Borghese; angel on Ponte Sant'Angelo; detail of the baldacchino, St. Peter's Basilica; David, Museo e Galleria Borghese; the colonnade, St. Peter's Square

Top Tips For…

These great suggestions will help you to create your ideal visit to Rome, no matter how you like to spend your time.

Burning the Midnight Oil
Sit up late with the beautiful people in **Ombre Rosse** (▷ 135).
Share a glass of wine with the characters in the bars around **Campo de' Fiori** (▷ 44–45).
Visit one or more of the many clubs in the **Testaccio** (▷ 130, 132) nightlife district.

Saving for a Rainy Day
Buy an integrated **travel pass** (▷ 167) and save on public transport.
Visit Rome's art-crammed churches, such as **Santa Maria sopra Minerva** (▷ 54–55): they are virtually all free.
Time your visit for the last Sunday of the month (9–12.30), when the expensive **Vatican Museums** (▷ 26–27) are free.

An Evening of Entertainment
See what's playing at the **Teatro dell'Opera di Roma** (▷ 137), Rome's opera house.
Enjoy a night of blues or jazz at the long-established **Big Mama** (▷ 133).
Look out for posters advertising **church recitals** and other **classical music concerts**. In summer, many are held outdoors (▷ 130).

Romantic Suppers
Dine outdoors in summer; try **Vecchia Roma** (▷ 151), but almost any restaurant or pizzeria with tables on a terrace will do.
Splash out on a meal at **Il Convivio Troiani** (▷ 145), for that special dining experience.
Buy a picnic and take it to the **Pincio** gardens (▷ 72) to watch the sun set over St. Peter's.

Specialty Shopping
Try **Via dei Coronari** (▷ panel, 120) and nearby streets for antiques and fabrics.

Clockwise from top left: Cafés in Piazza Navona buzz at night; ruined palaces on the Palatine Hill; dining at Giggetto in the Ghetto district; enjoy a coffee at

Stroll down **Via Margutta** to take in its various art galleries (▷ panel, 120).
For designer clothes and accessories, it has to be **Via dei Condotti** (▷ 120–121).

A Breath of Fresh Air
The **Villa Borghese** (▷ 75) park offers numerous walks and shady nooks.
Escape the crowds around the Forum by climbing the **Palatine Hill** (▷ 69–70).
If you don't have time to see the Gianicolo and Villa Doria Pamphilj above Trastevere, how about the closer **Orto Botanico** (▷ 61)?

A Taste of Tradition
Giggetto (▷ 147) and **Piperno** (▷ 149) serve classic Roman-Jewish cuisine.
As its name suggests, **Checchino dal 1887** (▷ 144–145) has been serving traditional Roman food for more than 120 years.
To sample pizza at its best, try **Ivo** (▷ 148) or **Da Baffetto** (▷ 145).

A Great Cup of Coffee
La Tazza d'Oro (▷ 151), just a stone's throw from the Pantheon, is a temple to the espresso.
Sant'Eustachio (▷ 150) serves what many consider to be Rome's best cup of coffee.
Antico Caffè del Brasile (▷ 142) knows its beans—Pope John Paul II once bought his coffee here.

The World's Best Classical Sculpture
Visit the **Palazzo Altemps** (▷ 34–35) and **Palazzo Massimo alle Terme** (▷ 40–41), which have beautifully presented collections.
To see individual sculptural works go to the **Musei Capitolini** (▷ 24–25), which has some of the city's most significant pieces.
The **Laocoön** (▷ 27) is the most celebrated of the Vatican Museums' immense collection of sculptures.

Sant'Eustachio; the head of Constantine in the Musei Capitolini; window-shop in style in Via dei Condotti; Bernini's elephant statue with the Pantheon behind

Timeline

753BC Traditional date of the foundation of Rome by Romulus, first of the city's seven kings.

616–578BC Tarquinius Priscus, Rome's first Etruscan king.

509BC Etruscans expelled and the Roman Republic founded.

60BC Rome ruled by a triumvirate of Pompey, Marcus Licinius Crassus and Julius Caesar.

PUNIC WARS

The First Punic War against Carthage (North Africa) started in 264BC and lasted for around 23 years. In the Second Punic War (218–201BC) Rome was threatened by Hannibal, leader of the Carthaginian army. But Rome finally defeated Carthage in the Third Punic War (149–146BC).

RELIGION

There are 280 churches within the city walls and 94 percent of Romans have had their children baptized. However, only 23 percent of Romans regularly attend Mass.

48BC Caesar declared ruler for life but assassinated by rivals in 44BC.

27BC–AD14 Rule of Octavian, Caesar's great nephew, who as Augustus becomes the first Roman emperor.

98–117 Reign of Emperor Trajan. Military campaigns extend the empire's boundaries.

284–286 Empire divided into East and West.

306–337 The Emperor Constantine reunites the Empire, legalizing Christianity. St. Peter's and the first Christian churches are built.

410 Rome is sacked by the Goths led by Alaric I.

476 Romulus Augustulus is the last Western Roman Emperor.

800 Charlemagne awards territories to the papacy; Pope Leo III crowns him Holy Roman Emperor.

The Arch of Constantine, on the route of the marathon in the 1960 Olympic Games

Gaius Julius Caesar

CAIUS JULIUS CÆSAR.

1508 Michelangelo begins the Sistine Chapel ceiling.

1527 Rome is sacked by German and Spanish troops under the Holy Roman Emperor, Charles V.

1848 Uprisings in Rome under Mazzini and Garibaldi force Pope Pius IX to flee. The new Roman Republic is defeated by the French in 1849 and the papacy restored.

1870 Rome joins a united Italy.

1929 Lateran Treaty recognizes the Vatican as a separate state.

1940 Italy enters World War II.

1960 Rome hosts the Olympic Games.

2000 Some 30 million pilgrims visit Rome for the millennial jubilee year.

2005 Pope John Paul II dies, after 26 years as pontiff, and is succeeded by Pope Benedict XVI.

2011 Technocrat Mario Monti is appointed Prime Minister.

2013 Argentinian Jorge Maria Bergoglio becomes Pope Francis I.

2017 Virginia Raggi, Rome's first female mayor, cancels the city's 2024 Olympic bid.

2019 Education minister Lorenzo Fioramonti urges schools to support pupils' climate strike action.

WHAT'S IN A NAME

Many of Rome's street names include dates that allude to significant events in the city's history. Via XX Settembre (September 20) commemorates the day in 1870 when Italian troops liberated Rome; the city became the country's capital in the same year. Via XXIV Maggio (May 24) recalls the day in 1915 that Italy entered World War I. Via IV Novembre (November 4) alludes to the date of the Italian armistice and victory in 1918 after World War I. And Via XXV Aprile (April 25) commemorates the day in 1944 when the Allies liberated the city from Nazi rule.

Detail of the ceiling of the Sistine Chapel painted by Michelangelo

Pope Francis I was elected in 2013

Top 25

This section contains the must-see Top 25 sights and experiences in Rome. They are listed alphabetically, and numbered so you can locate them on the inside front cover.

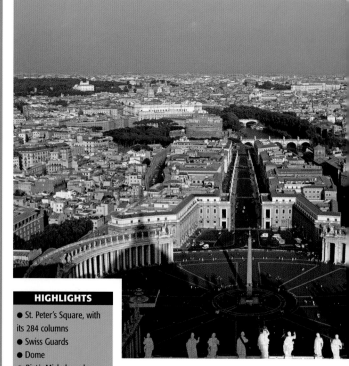

HIGHLIGHTS

● St. Peter's Square, with its 284 columns
● Swiss Guards
● Dome
● *Pietà,* Michelangelo
● The 25.5m (83ft) 13th-century BC Egyptian obelisk, brought here in the first century AD
● *St. Peter,* Arnolfo di Cambio
● Monument to Pope Alexander VII, Bernini

TIP

● You have to join what can be very long lines for security checks (on the right side of Piazza San Pietro) before entering the basilica. Arrive before 9am.

St. Peter's combines architecture, design, decoration, art and sculpture on a monumental scale, making this vast sacred complex a fitting spiritual capital for the world's millions of Catholics.

The creators The first St. Peter's was built by Constantine around AD326, reputedly on the site where St. Peter was buried following his crucifixion in AD64. By 1452 the church was in such a state of disrepair that Pope Nicholas V resolved to build a new basilica. After several false starts it was virtually rebuilt to plans by Bramante, and then again to designs by Antonio da Sangallo, Giacomo della Porta, Michelangelo and Carlo Maderno. Michelangelo was also responsible for much of the dome, and Bernini finished the facade and the interior.

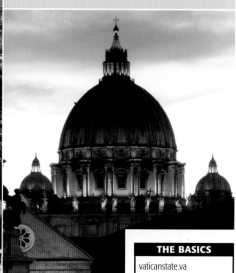

From left: The far-reaching views from the dome take in St. Peter's Square with its central obelisk, Bernini's impressive symmetrical colonnades and Rome beyond; the famous dome of St Peter's Basilica, designed by Michelangelo, is floodlit at night

What to see Michelangelo's unforgettable *Pietà* (1499)—which is behind glass following an attack in 1972—is in the first chapel of the right aisle. On the right side of the end of the nave stands a statue of St. Peter. His right foot has been caressed by millions of visitors and pilgrims since 1857, when Pius IX granted a 50-day indulgence to anyone kissing it following confession. Bernini's colossal sculpted bronze *baldacchino*, or high altar canopy (1624–33), was built during the papacy of Urban VIII, a scion of the Barberini family; it is decorated with bees, the Barberinis' dynastic symbol. Behind the altar are magnificent tombs, and under the basilica the grottoes contain the papal tombs. The view from the dome (the entrance is at the end of the right aisle, past the Holy Door) is a highlight of a visit.

THE BASICS

vaticanstate.va

✚ C4

✉ Piazza San Pietro, Città del Vaticano

☎ 06 6988 3731

🕐 Apr–Sep daily 7–7; Oct–Mar 7–6. Dome: Apr–Sep daily 7.30–6; Oct–Mar 7.30–5. Grottoes: Apr–Sep daily 7–6; Oct–Mar 7–5

🍴 Shop

Ⓜ Ottaviano

🚌 64 to Porta Cavalleggeri or 23, 32, 49, 492, 990 to Piazza del Risorgimento

♿ Wheelchair access

🎫 Basilica free. Dome moderate. Grottoes free

Castel Sant'Angelo, rising above the river, has served as an imperial tomb, a papal citadel, medieval prison and army barracks. Today the 58-room museum traces the castle's nearly 2,000-year history, providing a contrast to the Vatican Museums.

Many incarnations The Castel Sant'Angelo was built by Emperor Hadrian in AD130 as a mausoleum for himself, his family and his dynastic successors. It was crowned by a gilded chariot driven by a statue of Hadrian disguised as the sun god Apollo. Emperors were buried in its vaults until about AD271 when, under threat of invasion from Germanic raiders, it became a citadel and was incorporated into the city's walls. Its present name arose in AD590, after a vision by Gregory the Great, who, while leading

Clockwise from far left: The 18th-century statue atop the fortress is by Flemish sculptor Peter Anton von Verschaffelt; the building has been a mausoleum, fortress, papal prison and museum; Ponte Sant'Angelo, watched over by Bernini's angels; view of the Tiber from the terrace

a procession through Rome to pray for the end of plague, saw an angel sheathing a sword on this spot, an act thought to symbolize the end of the pestilence.

Castle and museum In 847 Leo IV converted the building into a papal fortress, and in 1277 Nicholas III linked it to the Vatican by a passageway, the *passetto*. Used as a prison in the Renaissance, and then an army barracks after 1870, the castle became a museum in 1933. Exhibits, spread over four floors, are scattered around a confusing but fascinating array of rooms and corridors. Best of these is the beautiful Sala Paolina, with stucco, fresco and trompe l'oeil decoration. The castle's terrace, granting a 360-degree view over the city, is the setting for the last act of Puccini's *Tosca*.

THE BASICS

castelsantangelo.
beniculturali.it

✚ E4

✉ Lungotevere Castello 50

☎ 06 681 9111 (Mon–Fri 9–6, Sat 9–1) for information and tickets, or online at gebart.it

🕐 Daily 9–7.30

🍴 Café

🚇 Lepanto

🚌 30, 49, 70, 87, 130, 492, 990 to Piazza Cavour or the Lungotevere

♿ Poor

💶 Expensive; free 1st Sun of month

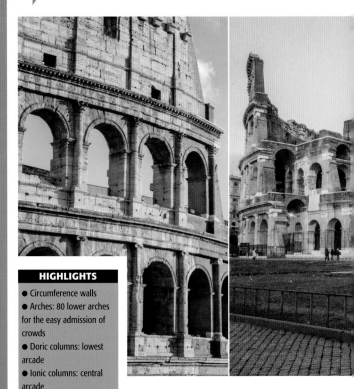

HIGHLIGHTS

- Circumference walls
- Arches: 80 lower arches for the easy admission of crowds
- Doric columns: lowest arcade
- Ionic columns: central arcade
- Corinthian columns: upper arcade
- Underground cells
- Sockets that once housed binding metal clamps
- *Vomitoria*: interior exits and entrances
- Views of ancient Rome from the upper levels

TIP

- The Colosseum's ticket office and security checks can be very busy—buy a timed entry ticket online to reduce waiting times.

No monument in Rome rivals the majesty of the Colosseum amphitheater, the largest surviving structure from Roman antiquity and the most popular tourist attraction in the world.

Awe-inspiring The Colosseum was begun by Emperor Vespasian in AD72 and inaugurated by his son, Titus, in AD80 with a gala that saw 5,000 animals slaughtered in a day (and 100 days of continuous games thereafter). Finishing touches to the 55,000-seat stadium were added by Domitian (AD81–96). Three types of columns support the arcades, and the walls are made of brick and volcanic tufa faced with marble blocks. Its long decline began in the Middle Ages, with the pillaging of stone to build churches and palaces. The desecration ended

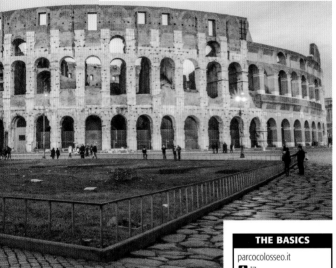

From left: The 80 arched entrances allowed easy access for the spectators; named after the Colossus of Nero statue, which stood nearby, the Colosseum had four stories of spectator seating, while underground was a maze of corridors, cells and animal pens

in 1744, when the structure was consecrated in memory of the Christians supposedly martyred in the arena (later research suggests they weren't). Clearing of the site and excavations began late in the 19th century.

Games Armed combat at the Colosseum went on for some 500 years. Criminals, slaves and gladiators fought each other or wild animals, often to the death, and mock sea battles were waged (the arena could be flooded via underground pipes). Spectators exercised the power of life and death over defeated combatants, by waving handkerchiefs to show mercy or displaying a down-turned thumb to demand the finishing stroke. Survivors' throats were often cut anyway, and the dead were poked with a red-hot iron to confirm their demise.

THE BASICS

parcocolosseo.it

✚ J7

✉ Piazza del Colosseo, Via dei Fori Imperiali

☎ 06 699 841; book online at coopculture.it

🕐 Mid-Feb to mid-Mar and Sep daily 8.30–6; Apr–Aug daily 8.30–7; Oct to mid-Feb daily 8.30–4.30

Ⓜ Colosseo

🚌 Tram 3; bus 75, 81, 87, 118 to Piazza del Colosseo

♿ Poor to the interior; limited access from Via Celio Vibenna entrance

💶 Expensive; joint ticket with Monte Palatino and Foro Romano; free 1st Sun of month

HIGHLIGHTS

- *Oceanus*
- *Allegory of Health* (right of *Oceanus*)
- *Virgin Indicating the Spring to Soldiers*
- *Allegory of Abundance* (left of *Oceanus*)
- *Agrippa Approving the Design of the Aqueduct*
- *Triton with Horse* (on the right, symbolizing the ocean in repose)
- *Triton with Horse* (on the left, symbolizing a tempestuous sea)
- Facade of Santi Vincenzo e Anastasio
- Baroque interior of Santa Maria in Trivio

A warren of narrow, cobbled streets leads east from the wide Via del Corso to disgorge you into a little piazza, almost entirely filled by the glorious sight and sound of one of Rome's most iconic fountains, the Fontana di Trevi.

Virgin discovery In its earliest guise the Trevi Fountain lay at the end of the Aqua Virgo, or Acqua Vergine, an aqueduct built by Agrippa in 19BC and supposedly filled with Rome's sweetest waters. The spring that fed it was reputedly discovered by a virgin, hence its name. She is said to have shown her discovery to some Roman soldiers, a scene—along with Agrippa's approval of the aqueduct's plans—described in bas-reliefs on the fountain's second tier. The fountain is dominated by the central figure of

Clockwise from left: The central figure of the fountain is Oceanus, god of the sea, in a chariot pulled by two winged horses; the fountain is particularly effective when floodlit at night; crowds gather to admire this impressive monument

Oceanus, his hair and robes streaming in the wind, who stands in a seashell chariot. This is drawn by two giant tritons, their horses symbolizing both calm and stormy seas. Other statues represent Abundance and Health and, above, the Four Seasons, which each carry gifts.

The fountains A new fountain was built in 1453, ordered by Pope Nicholas V, who paid for it by taxing wine. Its name came from the three roads *(tre vie)* that converged on the piazza. The present fountain was commissioned by Pope Clement XII in 1732 and finished in 1762. Its design was inspired by the Arch of Constantine and is attributed to Nicola Salvi, with possible contributions from Bernini. Those wishing to return to Rome toss a coin (over the shoulder) into the fountain.

THE BASICS

➕ G5

✉ Piazza Fontana di Trevi

🕐 Daily 24 hours

🚇 Spagna or Barberini

🚌 C3, 51, 53, 62, 63, 71, 80, 83, 117 and other routes to Via del Corso and Via del Tritone

♿ Access via cobbled street

💷 Free

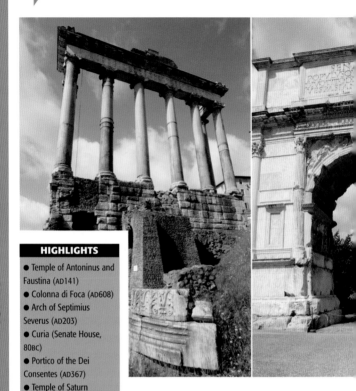

HIGHLIGHTS

● Temple of Antoninus and Faustina (AD141)
● Colonna di Foca (AD608)
● Arch of Septimius Severus (AD203)
● Curia (Senate House, 80BC)
● Portico of the Dei Consentes (AD367)
● Temple of Saturn (AD284)
● Santa Maria Antiqua, the Forum's oldest church, dating back to the fifth century AD
● Arch of Titus

TIPS

● Making sense of the Forum is quite a challenge. Use an audio guide to get more out of your visit.
● Take something to drink: there are no refreshments sold in the Forum area. There is also little shade.

The Roman Forum was the political and civic heart of the empire—the biggest and most important forum in the world—and even now it's an evocative ruin. It was here, according to Shakespeare, that Mark Antony delivered his "Friends, Romans, countrymen" speech after Caesar's assassination.

History The Forum (Foro Romano) started life as a marsh between the Palatine and Capitoline hills, taking its name from a word meaning "outside the walls." Later, it became a rubbish dump, then, when drained, a marketplace and religious shrine. In time it acquired all the structures of Rome's burgeoning civic, social and political life. Over the many centuries, consuls, emperors and senators embellished it with magnificent temples, courts and basilicas.

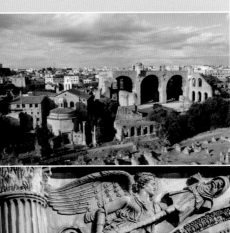

Clockwise from far left: Ionic columns mark the front of the Temple of Saturn; the triumphal Arch of Titus was built in the first century AD to commemorate the Emperor's sack of Jerusalem; climb the Palatine Hill for views over the Roman Forum; relief detail on the Arch of Septimius Severus

Forum Two millennia of plunder and decay have left a mishmash of odd pillars and jumbled stones, which nonetheless can begin to make vivid sense given a plan and some imagination. The Rostrum, the setting for Mark Antony's famous speech, provided the platform for many great historic moments.

Beauty spots Today, orange trees, oleanders and cypresses line the paths, and grasses and wildflowers flourish among the ancient remains. Somewhat aloof from the rubble stands the elegantly restored House of the Vestal Virgins (Casa delle Vestali), home of a group of daughters of the Roman nobility chosen to serve Vesta, goddess of hearth and home. There were always six in number, and they served for 30 years, from age six to 36.

THE BASICS

parcocolosseo.it

�� H7

✉ Entrance at Largo Romolo e Remo on Via dei Fori Imperiali

☎ Book online at coopculture.it

🕐 As Colosseum (▷ 19)

Ⓜ Colosseo

🚌 51, 85, 87, 117, 118 to Via dei Fori Imperiali

♿ Access difficult

💲 Expensive; joint ticket with Colosseo and Palatino

HIGHLIGHTS

Palazzo Nuovo
● Replica equestrian piazza statue of Marcus Aurelius
● *Capitoline Venus*: life-size statue of the goddess
● The colossal statue of river god Marforio above the fountain in the courtyard

Palazzo dei Conservatori
● Caravaggio's painting of St. John the Baptist
● Bronze of *Lupa Capitolina*
● The original, restored statue of Marcus Aurelius
● Giant head and fragments of Constantine's statue

TIP

● The top-floor café, accessible without paying the museum entrance fee, offers wonderful views of the city.

The superb Greek and Roman sculptures in the Capitoline Museums (Palazzo Nuovo and Palazzo dei Conservatori) make a far more accessible introduction to the field than the Vatican Museums.

Palazzo Nuovo The Capitoline Museums occupy two palaces on opposite sides of the Piazza del Campidoglio and are linked by an underground passage. Designed by Michelangelo, the Palazzo Nuovo (on the north side) contains most of the finest pieces. The focus of the beautiful piazza is a magnificent equestrian bronze statue of the philosophical emperor Marcus Aurelius, a replica of the second-century original, which is now housed, after a superb restoration, in a purpose-built space inside the museum. Among the other

Clockwise from far left: The remains of Constantine's giant statue, displayed in the courtyard, include the head and a hand; the Dying Gaul, a wonderful example of classical sculpture; visitors admiring a bust of Constantine and frescoes; the Etruscan bronze of Romulus and Remus

sculptures inside the museum are celebrated Roman copies in marble of Greek originals, including the *Dying Gaul*, *Wounded Amazon*, *Capitoline Venus* and the discus thrower *Discobolus*. In the Sala degli Imperatori is a portrait gallery of busts of Roman emperors.

Palazzo dei Conservatori As well as the Pinacoteca Capitolina art gallery and original Marcus Aurelius statue, the Conservatori is distinguished by a courtyard featuring the head and fragments of the fourth-century AD statue of Constantine, originally 12m (40ft) high. Also inside is the fifth-century BC Etruscan *Lupa Capitolina*, the she-wolf suckling Romulus and Remus (the twins were added by Antonio Pollaiuolo in 1510). Paintings include works by Caravaggio, Velázquez, Titian and Veronese.

THE BASICS

museicapitolini.org

✚ G6

✉ Piazza del Campidoglio 1 (ticket office in Palazzo dei Conservatori)

☎ 06 0608; book online at ticket.museiin comuneroma.it

🕐 Daily 9.30–7.30

🚌 40, 44, 64 and all other services to Piazza Venezia

♿ Poor: ramped steps to Piazza del Campidoglio. Telephone in advance (06 6710 2071) for help

💶 Expensive; combined Capitolini Card available; free 1st Sun of month

HIGHLIGHTS

● Michelangelo's fearsome depiction of God in the *Creation of Adam* in the Sistine Chapel
● *Apollo del Belvedere* (Museo Pio-Clementino)
● *Marte di Todi* (Museo Gregoriano-Etrusco)
● Maps Gallery (Galleria delle Carte Geografiche)
● Paintings in the Pinacoteca (Art Gallery)
● Room of the Animals (Museo Pio-Clementino)

TIPS

● Avoid waiting in long lines to get in by booking your tickets online at museivaticani.va.
● Don't become trapped in the lines to see the Sistine Chapel—decide beforehand on your own priorities.

This is the largest, most impressive museum complex in the world, and includes one of Michelangelo's supreme masterpieces in the Sistine Chapel.

Treasures of 12 museums At least two days (and 7km/4 miles of walking) are needed to do justice to the Vatican Museums. Egyptian and Assyrian art; Etruscan artifacts; the more esoteric anthropological collections; or modern religious art—whatever your priorities, several sights should not be missed. Most obvious are the four rooms of the Stanze di Raffaello, each of which is decorated with frescoes by Raphael. Further fresco cycles by Pinturicchio and Fra Angelico adorn the Borgia Apartment and Chapel of Nicholas V, and are complemented by an almost unmatched collection of paintings

Clockwise from far left: Giuseppe Momo's spiral staircase; the Laocoön group in the Museo Pio-Clementino; Michelangelo's ceiling in the Sistine Chapel; the decorated ceiling of the Galleria della Carte Geografiche; detail of a fresco by Melozzo da Forlì in the Pinacoteca

in the Vatican Art Gallery. The best of the Greek and Roman sculpture is the breathtaking Laocoön group in the Cortile Ottagono of the Museo Pio-Clementino. The list of artists whose work is shown in the Collezione di Arte Religiosa Moderna is a roll call of the most famous in the last 100 years, from Pablo Picasso to Salvador Dalí and Henry Moore.

Sistine Chapel The chapel was built for Pope Sixtus IV between 1475 and 1483, but Pope Julius II commissioned Michelangelo to paint the ceiling in 1508. The frescoes, comprising more than 300 individual figures, were completed in four years. The extraordinary fresco behind the high altar, the *Last Judgment*, was begun for Pope Paul III in 1534 and completed in 1541.

THE BASICS

museivaticani.va

➕ C4

✉ Viale Vaticano 100, Città del Vaticano

☎ 06 6988 4676

🕐 Mon–Sat 9–6 (ticket office closes at 4); last Sun of month 9–2 (ticket office closes 12.30)

🍴 Café, restaurant and shop

Ⓜ Cipro–Musei Vaticani

🚌 Tram 19; bus 23, 32, 49, 81, 492, 990 to Piazza del Risorgimento, 40 to Piazza Pia or 64 to Porta Cavalleggeri

♿ Wheelchair access

💵 Very expensive (includes entry to all Vatican museums); free last Sun of month (9–12.30)

27

8 Museo dei Fori Imperiali e Mercati di Traiano

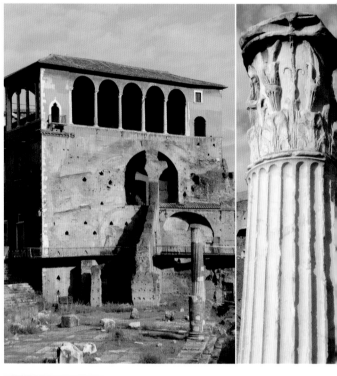

HIGHLIGHTS

- The view of the 13th-century Torre delle Milizie
- The intricate spiral bas-relief that climbs Trajan's Column, depicting victories in battle
- The Basilica Ulpia, which played an important role in the Imperial City, dedicated not only to religion but also to justice

Rome's classical history is continually being revealed, and there's nowhere better to take in 21st-century archaeological discoveries than at this fascinating museum and the surrounding excavated area.

Trajan's Markets The Mercati di Traiano were originally regarded as the precursor of modern shopping malls—a group of commercial buildings constructed in the second century AD as a semicircular range of halls on three levels. Two of the levels survive in excellent condition. It's now thought, however, that the "markets" were in fact probably a new hub for politics and justice inaugurated by the Emperor Trajan in AD112, some five years before his death. The 150 or so booths and halls of the structure would have been administrative offices

Clockwise from far left: The large complex known as Trajan's Markets, where Romans gathered to conduct business; a lone column by the 13th-century Torre delle Milizie; shop fronts in Trajan's Markets; carved reliefs on Trajan's Column recall the emperor's battles

populated by civil servants, though some at ground level may have been shops. Either way, they present a magnificent spectacle.

Museum The labyrinthine museum within Trajan's Markets offers an absorbing peep into Rome's past. It presents the grand Imperial Fora using modern techniques, including film and pictographic illustration, and displays items unearthed in recent excavations in the area. The external viewing gallery gives a splendid view, not only of the surrounding ruins, but the whole Fora area of ancient Rome, as well as the AD113 Trajan's Column, which stands at 30m (100ft).

The Museo dei Fori Imperiali is also a venue for contemporary arts, with regular displays of paintings and specially convened exhibitions.

THE BASICS

mercatiditraiano.it

➕ H6

✉ Via IV Novembre 94

☎ 06 0608; book online at ticket.museiin comuneroma.it

🕐 Daily 9.30–7.30 (last admission 1 hour before closing)

🚇 Cavour

🚌 H, 40, 64, 70, 117, 170 and other routes to Via IV Novembre

♿ Good

💶 Expensive

● Antonio Canova's fine sculpture of Paolina Borghese (1804), who was Napoleon's sister and the wife of Camillo Borghese. She is shown bare-breasted and looks every bit as seductive in marble as she was in real life.
● The Bernini sculptures
● The Caravaggio paintings
● Titian's *Sacred and Profane Love*
● Raphael's *Deposition of Christ*
● The interior decoration

The Galleria Borghese may be small, but what it lacks in quantity it more than makes up for in quality. The gallery combines paintings and sculptures, including many masterpieces by Gian Lorenzo Bernini, Raphael, Caravaggio and others.

Bernini sculptures The Villa Borghese was designed in 1613 as a summer retreat for Cardinal Scipione Borghese, nephew of Pope Paul V, who accumulated most of the collection (acquired by the state in 1902). Scipione was an enthusiastic patron of Bernini, whose works dominate one floor of the gallery. His *David* (1623–24) is said to be a self-portrait, while *Apollo and Daphne* (1622–25), in the next room, is considered his masterpiece. Other Bernini works include the *Rape of Proserpina*

From far left: Canova's reclining statue of Paolina Borghese is a highlight of the gallery; Bernini's Rape of Proserpina depicting Proserpina, Pluto (the god of the underworld) and Cerberus, the three-headed dog (the guardian of the underworld); Boy with a Fruit Basket by Caravaggio

(1622) and *Truth Unveiled by Time* (1652). The statues are complemented by some of Rome's most beautifully decorated rooms.

The setting The museum is in the grounds of the Villa Borghese (▷ 75), north of the city. It is Rome's largest public park—80ha (200 acres) with five museums, gardens, lakes, fountains and a deer park. Before Cardinal Scipione made the grounds the base of his 17th-century pleasure palace, they were vineyards.

The paintings Foremost in this collection are works by Raphael *(The Deposition of Christ,* 1507), Titian *(Sacred and Profane Love,* 1512*)*, Caravaggio *(Boy with a Fruit Basket* and *Madonna dei Palafrenieri,* 1605*)* and Correggio *(Danaë,* 1530*)*.

THE BASICS

galleriaborghese.
beniculturali.it

✚ J2

✉ Piazzale Scipione Borghese 5

☎ 06 841 3979; advance tickets available online only (gebart.it)

🕐 Tue–Sun 9–7

Ⓢ Spagna or Flaminio

🚌 63, 92, 223, 360 to Via Po, or 53, 910 to Via Pinciana, or C3 to Via delle Belle Arti

♿ Steps to front entrance

💰 Very expensive

31

HIGHLIGHTS

● The Museum
● Piazzale della Corporazione
● The Baths of Neptune
● Casa di Diana

TIPS

● Allow a whole day for the site; perhaps bring a picnic.
● In summer, take water with you and rest in the shade during the early afternoon.
● Buy a plan of the site and spend time when you arrive planning your visit.

Imperial Rome's port of Ostia is one of the best-preserved Roman towns in Italy. Come here to get a real sense of everyday Roman life, in a peaceful setting amid pine trees.

Living history Less celebrated than Pompeii or Herculaneum, Ostia Antica more than rivals its sisters. Lying 25km (15 miles) southwest of Rome, its 4,000ha (10,000-acre) pastoral setting is equal to Italy's most glorious country-side. Located on the Tiber, the port town was Rome's trade link with the outside world for 600 years, until a receding coastline and imperial decline hastened its demise. By the 17th century Ostia was all but forgotten. Legend claims it was founded by the Etruscans in the seventh century BC—but archaeological dating places it in the fourth century BC.

From left: Detail of the remains of a Corinthian capital, displayed at the archaeological site; the fine remnants, including the amphitheater, at this well-preserved Roman town give a good impression of what everyday life was like in an ancient port city

THE BASICS

ostiaantica.
beniculturali.it (online tickets)

➕ See map ▷ 114

✉ Viale dei Romagnoli 717

☎ 06 5635 0215

🕐 Apr–Aug Tue–Sun 8.30–7.15 (last admission 6.15); Sep 8.30–7 (last admission 6); Oct 8.30–6.30 (last admission 5.30); Nov to mid-Feb 8.30–4.30 (last admission 3.30); mid-Feb to mid-Mar 8.30–4 (last admission 3); mid-Mar to last Sat Mar 8.30–5.30 (last admission 4.30); closed public holidays

🍽 Restaurant

🚇 Metro line B to Piramide, then train from adjoining Roma–Lido station (covered by BIG ticket, ▷ panel 167)

💰 Moderate; free 1st Sun of month

The site What we see today is only about half of the town, uncovered by archaeological excavations that began in the 19th century and continue today—a major new area north of the Tiber was discovered at the end of 2019. Pride of place goes to the vast 4,000-seat amphitheater, which is still used for open-air concerts in the summer. There are remarkable discoveries all along and off the main road, Decumanus Maximus, which is rutted where laden carts once carried goods to and from the great port. Surrounded by Aleppo pines and cedars are the remains of the Forum, a second-century AD multistory apartment block called the Casa di Diana, the Baths of Neptune with its splendid mosaics, and the Piazzale della Corporazione, the original business district, flanked by remains of shops, offices and *horrea* (warehouses).

HIGHLIGHTS

- Aphrodite's throne
- *Galatian Soldier* statue
- Courtyard loggia
- Statue of Orestes and Electra embracing in a fond farewell

TIP

- The Palazzo Altemps is easily seen in conjunction with Piazza Navona. But note that its sister museum, the Palazzo Massimo alle Terme, is a long way away, by Termini Station.

This beautiful building epitomizes the best of Renaissance urban architecture, while its elegant rooms provide the setting for some of the finest of Rome's Classical sculpture.

The building Rome's Museo Nazionale Romano (National Roman Museum) is housed in two superbly restored buildings: the Palazzo Massimo alle Terme (▷ 40–41) near the station and here in the Palazzo Altemps, whose odd-sounding name is the Italian corruption of the German name von Hohenemps. Designed by Melozzo da Forlì, and mainly constructed in the 15th century, the building houses a series of charming and intimate rooms, many with vaulted ceilings. One gives access to a splendidly frescoed loggia overlooking the comings and goings of a harmonious inner courtyard.

Clockwise from far left: The statue of Orestes and Electra; elegant rooms provide a superb backdrop for the collections; the Ludovisi Throne shows Aphrodite being plucked from the sea; statues watch over the Palazzo Altemps's peaceful inner courtyard

The best time to get a sense of the building's history is as dusk falls, when the rooms and exhibits are imaginatively lit.

The collections The palazzo is home to the Ludovisi Collection, amassed by Cardinal Ludovico Ludovisi in the 17th century, as well as a collection of Egyptian antiques and portraits. Downstairs is the *Tiber Apollo*, found in the bed of the river in the late 19th century, and two gigantic statues of Athena. Upstairs, the star of the collection, the fifth-century BC Ludovisi Throne, is probably a Greek sculpture dedicated as a throne for Aphrodite. The delicate carving portrays the goddess rising from the sea. Don't miss the statue of the *Galatian Soldier and His Wife Committing Suicide*, apparently commissioned by Julius Caesar.

THE BASICS

coopculture.it

✚ F5

✉ Piazza di Sant' Apollinare 46

☎ 06 684851 (information) or 06 3996 7700 (ticket office); book online at coopculture.it

🕐 Tue–Sun 9–7.45

🚍 70, 81, 87, 116T, 186, 492, 628 to Corso del Rinascimento

♿ Moderate; combined ticket with Palazzo Massimo, Crypta Balbi and Terme di Diocleziano

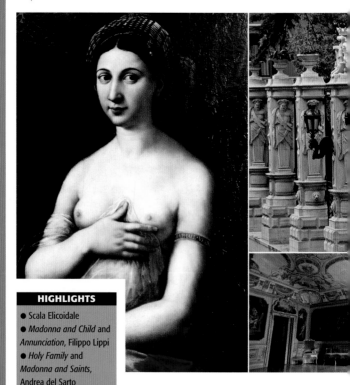

HIGHLIGHTS

● Scala Elicoidale
● *Madonna and Child* and *Annunciation*, Filippo Lippi
● *Holy Family* and *Madonna and Saints*, Andrea del Sarto
● *Madonna and Child*, Beccafumi
● Borromini's false-perspective window on the top floor
● *Adoration of the Shepherds* and *Baptism of Christ*, El Greco
● *Judith and Holofernes* and *Narciso*, Caravaggio
● *Beatrice Cenci*, attributed to Guido Reni
● *Henry VIII*, attributed to Holbein
● *The Triumph of Divine Providence*, Pietro da Cortona (Gran Salone)

The magnificent Palazzo Barberini, designed by Bernini, Borromini and Carlo Maderno, houses a stupendous ceiling fresco and one of Rome's finest art collections, the Galleria Nazionale d'Arte Antica.

Pope Urban The palace was commissioned by Maffeo Barberini for his family when he became Pope Urban VIII in 1623. It was begun by Carlo Maderno and completed by Bernini. The epitome of Rome's high baroque style, it is a maze of sumptuous suites, apartments and staircases. Overshadowing all is the Gran Salone, dominated by Pietro da Cortona's rich ceiling frescoes (1639), glorifying Urban as an agent of Divine Providence. The central windows and oval spiral staircase (Scala Elicoidale) are the work of Borromini.

Clockwise from far left: Raphael's *La Fornarina* forms part of the art collection; wrought-iron railings supported by decorative columns in the grounds of the palazzo; Judith and Holofernes by Caravaggio; the exterior of Palazzo Barberini; frescoes outlined in gold adorn the walls and ceiling

The collection *Antica* here means old rather than ancient. Probably the most popular painting in the collection is Raphael's *La Fornarina* (also attributed to Giulio Romano). It is said to be a portrait of one of the artist's several mistresses, identified later as the daughter of a *fornaio* (baker). It was executed in the year of the painter's death, a demise brought on, it is said, by his mistress's unrelenting passion. Elsewhere, eminent Italian works from Filippo Lippi, Andrea del Sarto, Caravaggio and Guido Reni stand alongside works by leading foreign artists, such as Holbein (a portrait of Henry VIII, dressed for his wedding to Anne of Cleves) and El Greco (a Nativity and the *Baptism of Christ*). Also here is a splendid collection of furniture, ceramics and other beautiful examples of the decorative arts.

THE BASICS

barberinicorsini.org

✚ J4

✉ Via delle Quattro Fontane 13

☎ 06 481 4591; book online at tosc.it

🕐 Tue–Sun 8.30–7

Ⓜ Barberini

🚌 52, 53, 58, 60, 61, 95, 116, 175, 492, 590 to Via Nazionale or Via del Tritone

♿ Few

💶 Moderate; combined ticket with Palazzo Corsini (▶ 71) moderate, valid for 3 days

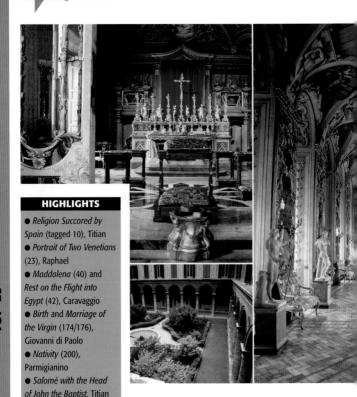

TOP 25

TIPS

● Use the audio guide, which is included in the price and helps make sense of what you're seeing.
● The paintings are not well lit so it is better to visit during daylight hours.

This is one of Rome's largest palaces and contains one of the city's finest patrician art collections. It also offers the chance to admire some of the sumptuously decorated rooms of its private apartments.

A dynasty Little in the bland exterior of the Palazzo Doria Pamphilj prepares you for the glory of the beautiful rooms that lie within. The core of the building was erected in 1435, and it has withstood countless alterations and owners. The Doria Pamphilj dynasty was formed by the union of the Doria, a famous Genoese seafaring clan, and the Pamphilj, a noble Roman family. Most people come here for the paintings, accessed through the State Apartments. These five lavish and superbly decorated salons open out from each other

Clockwise from far left: The family chapel has an elaborate marble altar; inside, the galleries are lavishly decorated with painted ceilings and the walls adorned with ornate mirrors; Salomé with the Head of John the Baptist by Titian; a cool oasis of green—one of the palace's five inner courtyards

to reach the ballroom, with its gold and white stucco, mirrors, chandeliers and silk-hung walls. Beyond is the private chapel (1690) and the entrance to the picture galleries.

Labyrinth of masterpieces The Pamphilj's art collection is displayed in ranks in four broad galleries. As the works are numbered, not labeled, it's worth investing in a guidebook from the ticket office. The finest painting—which has a room to itself—is the famous Velázquez portrait, *Innocent X* (1650), a likeness that captured the pope's weak and suspicious nature so adroitly that Innocent is said to have lamented that it was "too true, too true." It was Innocent's nephew Camillo Pamphilj who acquired the palazzo through his marriage to Olimpia Borghese in 1647.

THE BASICS

doriapamphilj.it

➕ G5

✉ Via del Corso 305

☎ 06 679 7323

🕐 Daily 9–7 (last admission 6); plus evening concerts (expensive) when gallery can be viewed

🍴 Café-bar on ground floor

🚌 C3, 51, 62, 63, 80, 83, 85 to Via del Corso or services to Piazza Venezia

♿ Good

💶 Expensive

- *Niobid from the Hortus Sallustiani* (Room VIII)
- The collection of coins in the basement
- *The Sleeping Hermaphrodite* (Room VII)
- House of Livia (Room II)
- The Villa Farnesina (Gallery II, Rooms III–V)

TIP

- The combined ticket is also valid for three days for all parts of the Museo Nazionale Romano, notably the Palazzo Altemps.

This sublime collection of Greek and Roman sculpture, with outstanding and unique displays of ancient Roman wall paintings and mosaics, dates from the end of the Republican age to the late Imperial age.

The building The Palazzo Massimo is an elegant and airy palace that has been beautifully renovated. The palace, which was designed by Camillo Pistrucci, was built in the late 19th century by the Massimo family to replace an earlier one demolished to make way for Termini station. In 1981 the palace was acquired by the state, and in the 1990s it was transformed into one of Rome's most attractive museums. There are four floors of museum space, a modern library, a conference room and a computer-based documentation area.

Clockwise from far left: A pavement mosaic of the head of Pan forms part of the displays; a fourth-century BC marble inlay panel; the Lancellotti Discobolus (Discus Thrower) is one of the masterpieces in the collection; intricate patterns frame this third-century BC mosaic of Dionysus

The collection This is one of two buildings (the other being the Palazzo Altemps, ▷ 34–35) housing Rome's magnificent Classical collections. Here you'll find some of the city's greatest treasures, from naked gods and games players to sarcophagi and goddesses. Don't miss the portrait busts or the wonderful Roman frescoes and mosaics on the upper floor.

Lancellotti Discobolus This fine marble copy of the great *Discus Thrower* dates from the mid-second century AD, and is one of the most famous copies of a fifth-century BC work. Discovered in the 18th century, it was sent to Germany during World War II and returned in 1948. It reproduces an original bronze that was probably the work of Myron, a Greek sculptor renowned for his portraits of athletes.

THE BASICS

coopculture.it

⊞ K5

✉ Piazza dei Cinquecento 67–Largo di Villa Peretti 1

☎ Reservations 06 3996 7701; book online at coopculture.it

🕐 Tue–Sun 9–7.45

🚇 Termini or Repubblica

🚍 All services to Termini and Piazza dei Cinquecento

♿ Moderate; combined ticket with Palazzo Altemps, Crypta Balbi and Terme di Diocleziano

HIGHLIGHTS

● Facade inscription
● Pedimented portico
● Original Roman doors
● Marble interior and pavement
● Coffered dome and oculus
● Tomb of Raphael
● Royal tombs

TIP

● The Pantheon is often very crowded. To make the most of your visit, go on a weekday or early in the morning.

No other monument suggests the grandeur of ancient Rome as much as this temple, whose early conversion to a place of Christian worship ensured the survival of a complete Roman imperial monument.

Temple and church The greatest surviving complete Roman structure, built by Emperor Hadrian in AD118–28, the Pantheon replaced a temple of 27BC by Marcus Agrippa, son-in-law of Augustus. (Modestly, Hadrian retained the original inscription proclaiming it as Agrippa's work.) It became the church of Santa Maria ad Martyres in AD609 (the bones of martyrs were brought here from the Catacombs) and is now a shrine to Italy's "immortals," including the artist Raphael and kings Vittore Emanuele II and Umberto I.

Clockwise from left: Visitors gaze at the interior where massive Egyptian granite columns support the dome; the sun pours in through the oculus, an opening in the Pantheon's roof; the Pantheon borders Piazza della Rotonda and its fountain by Giacomo della Porta

An engineering marvel Massive and simple from the outside, the Pantheon is at its most breathtaking inside, where the scale, harmony and symmetry of the dome in particular are more apparent. The world's largest dome until 1882 (when it was surpassed in the English spa resort of Buxton), it has a diameter of 43.3m (142ft)—equal to its height from the floor. Weight and stresses were reduced by rows of coffers in the ceiling, and the use of progressively lighter materials from the base to the crown. The central oculus, 9m (30ft) in diameter and clearly intended to inspire meditation on the heavens above, lets light (and rain) fall onto the marble pavement far below. Relax in one of Piazza della Rotonda's cafés to enjoy and admire the exterior view of the Pantheon and the atmosphere of the piazza.

THE BASICS

pantheonroma.com

➕ F5

✉ Piazza della Rotonda

☎ 347 820 5204

🕐 Mon–Sat 8.30–7.30, Sun 9–6, public holidays 9–1

🚌 116, 119 to Piazza della Rotonda or 40, 64, 70 and all other services to Largo di Torre Argentina

♿ Good

✋ Free

HIGHLIGHTS

● Street market
● Statue of Giordano Bruno marking where the philosopher was martyred for heresy in 1600
● Piazza della Cancelleria
● Palazzo Pio Righetti
● Santa Maria dell'Orazione e Morte: church door decorated with stone skulls
● The inscription on the "new" La Terrina (Tureen) fountain: "Do well and let them talk"

Few places in Rome are more relaxing to sit and watch the world go by than Campo de' Fiori, a lovely old piazza whose fruit, vegetable and fish market makes it one of the liveliest and most vivid corners of the old city.

Ancient square In the Middle Ages, Piazza Campo de' Fiori, or the Field of Flowers, was turned from a meadow facing the ancient Theater of Pompey (55BC; now the Palazzo Pio Righetti) into one of the city's most exclusive residential and business districts. By the 15th century it was surrounded by busy inns and bordellos, some run by the infamous courtesan Vannozza Cattanei, mistress of Pope Alexander VI. By February 1600 it had also become a place of execution, the fate of Giordano Bruno,

Clockwise from far left: A selection of squashes for sale at the market; at night the bars and cafés are popular meeting places; a string of red chilies adorns a market stall; crates of fresh fruit and vegetables are brought to the market; stalls display their colorful produce

a Dominican priest and philospher who was burned alive for heresy. His cowled statue stands at the center of the piazza.

Present day Just sit back and soak up the atmosphere. Students, visitors and locals mingle with market vendors shouting their wares, while the cafés, bars market stalls and bakeries will have you relishing the street life. One block south lies Piazza Farnese, dominated by the Palazzo Farnese, a Renaissance master-piece partly designed by Michelangelo and begun in 1516. It is now home to the French Embassy. One block west is the Palazzo della Cancelleria (1485), once the papal chancellery. The nearby Via Giulia, Via dei Baullari, Via dei Cappellari and Via del Pellegrino are wonderful streets to explore.

THE BASICS

✚ F6

✉ Piazza Campo de' Fiori

🕐 Market Mon–Sat 7–1.30

🚌 40, 46, 62, 64 to Corso Vittorio Emanuele II or C3, H, 40, 42, 62, 64, 70, 81, 87 to Largo di Torre Argentina

♿ Cobbled streets and some curbs around piazza

🆓 Free

TOP 25

HIGHLIGHTS

● Fontana dei Quattro Fiumi (center)
● Fontana del Moro (south)
● Fontana del Nettuno (north)
● Palazzo Pamphilj
● San Luigi dei Francesi (Via Santa Giovanna d'Arco)
● Santa Maria dell'Anima (Via della Pace)

Piazza Navona, with its atmospheric echoes of a 2,000-year history, is a glorious place to wander through or stop for a drink at a sun-drenched table and watch the world go by.

Shaping history Piazza Navona owes its unmistakable elliptical shape to a stadium and racetrack built here in AD86 by Emperor Domitian. From the Circus Agonalis—the stadium for athletic games—comes the piazza's present name, rendered in medieval Latin as *in agone*, and then in Rome's strangulated dialect as *'n 'agona*. The stadium was used until well into the Middle Ages for festivals and competitions, as well as a market. The square owes its present baroque appearance to rebuilding by Pope Innocent X (reigned 1644–1655), whose palace stood on the square.

Clockwise from far left: Bernini's Fontana dei Quattro Fiumi is the largest fountain in Piazza Navona; the piazza at night; sculptural detail on the Fontana dei Quattro Fiumi; elegant cafés and restaurants line the square; passing the time of day beside the Fontana del Moro in the south of the square

Around the piazza Bernini's spirited Fontana dei Quattro Fiumi (Fountain of the Four Rivers) dominates. Unveiled in 1651, it has four figures that represent the four rivers of Paradise (the Nile, Ganges, Danube and Plate), and the four "corners" of the world (Africa, Asia, Europe and America). On the west side of the piazza is the baroque Sant' Agnese in Agone (1652–57), its facade designed by Borromini. Bernini's river gods are said to recoil in horror from his rival's work. Beside the church stands the Palazzo Pamphilj, commissioned by Pope Innocent X and now the Brazilian Embassy. Farther afield, San Luigi dei Francesi is famous for three super-lative Caravaggio paintings (in the rear chapel of the left nave), and Santa Maria della Pace for a cloister by Bramante and Raphael's frescoes of the four *Sybils*.

THE BASICS

- 🔳 F5
- ✉ Piazza Navona
- 🚇 Spagna
- 🚌 30, 70, 81, 87, 130, 492, 628 to Corso del Rinascimento or 40, 46, 62, 64 to Corso Vittorio Emanuele II
- ♿ Good

HIGHLIGHTS

- Spanish Steps
- Museo Keats-Shelley (▷ 70)
- Trinità dei Monti
- Fontana della Barcaccia
- Babington's Tea Rooms
- Villa Medici gardens
- Pincio gardens (▷ 72)

TIP

- Sitting down on the steps was banned by the city authorities in 2019 to protect the marble. Violators risk an on-the-spot fine.

The Piazza di Spagna lies at the foot of the Spanish Steps, a sinuous curve rising to the Trinità dei Monti. Streams of visitors come to enjoy the views and the atmosphere.

Spanish Steps Known in English as the Spanish Steps, in Italian this beautiful stairway gets its name, the Scalinata di Trinità dei Monti, from the French-owned church at the top. They were commissioned and built in 1723 with funds bequeathed by Etienne Gueffier, the French ambassador, to link the church with the piazza, itself named for the Spanish embassy that stood here a century earlier.

Around the steps At the base of the steps is the Fontana della Barcaccia, commissioned in 1627 by Pope Urban VIII and designed either

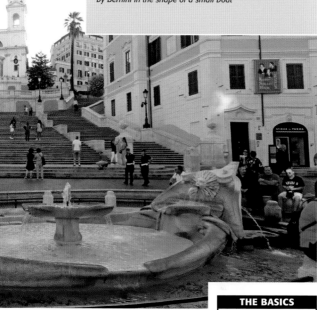

From left: The graceful church of Trinità dei Monti at the top of the Spanish Steps; at the bottom of the steps in the Piazza di Spagna is the Fontana della Barcaccia, designed by Bernini in the shape of a small boat

by Gian Lorenzo Bernini or by his less famous father, Pietro. The eccentric design represents a half-sunken boat. As you face the steps from below, to your right stands the Museo Keats-Shelley (▶ 70), with its fascinating collection of literary memorabilia and a working library, housed in the lodgings where the poet John Keats died in 1821, aged 25. At the top of the steps you can enjoy views past the magnificent Palazzo Barberini (▶ 36–37) and towards the Quirinal Hill; walk into the simple Trinità dei Monti church, with its double exterior stairs by Domenico Fontana and its frescoed chapels; and visit the beautiful gardens of the 16th-century Villa Medici, the seat of the French Academy in Rome, where French scholars come to study painting, sculpture, architecture, engraving and music.

THE BASICS

✚ G4

✉ Piazza di Spagna

☎ Villa Medici 06 676 1311; villamedici.it. Trinità dei Monti 06 679 4179

🕐 Spanish Steps daily 24 hours. Trinità dei Monti Mon, Wed, Thu 10.15–7, Fri 12–9, Sat 9.15–9, Sun 9–8. Villa Medici guided visits Tue–Sun (call for English-language tours)

🍴 Babington's Tea Rooms

Ⓜ Spagna

🚌 117 to Piazza di Spagna

🚫 None

🎟 Free

HIGHLIGHTS

- Choir screen
- Chapel of St. Catherine: fresco cycle
- *Ciborio* (altar canopy)
- Apse mosaic: *The Triumph of the Cross*
- Monument to Cardinal Roverella, Giovanni Dalmata (upper church)
- Fresco: *Miracle of San Clemente* (upper church)
- Fresco: *Legend of Sisinnio* (lower church)
- *Triclinium*
- Altar of Mithras: bas-relief of Mithras slaying the bull

No site in Rome reveals the layers of history that underpin the city as vividly as this beautiful medieval ensemble. It is built over a superbly preserved fourth-century church and the remains of a third-century Roman Mithraic temple.

The upper church The present San Clemente, which was named after Rome's fourth pope, was built between 1108 and 1184 to replace an earlier church that was sacked by the Normans in 1084. Almost untouched since, its medieval interior is dominated by the 12th-century marble panels of the choir screen and pulpits and the glittering 12th-century apse mosaic, *The Triumph of the Cross*. Equally captivating are the *Life of St. Catherine* frescoes (1428–31) by Masolino da Panicale.

Clockwise from far left: The 12th-century choir and altar in the upper church; exploring the excavated levels below the present church; detail of Masolino's Crucifixion fresco; the plain exterior of San Clemente; the decorated altar of Mithras is flanked by stone benches

Below ground Steps descend to the lower church, which retains traces of 8th- to 11th-century frescoes of San Clemente and the legends of St. Alessio and St. Sisinnio. More steps lead deeper into the twilight world of the best-preserved of the 12 Mithraic temples uncovered in Rome. (Mithraism was a popular, men-only cult that orginated in Persia—modern Iran—but was later eclipsed by Christianity.) Here are an altar with a bas-relief of Mithras ritually slaying a bull, and the *triclinium*, used for banquets and rites. Ongoing excavations are revealing parts of the temple, the Mithraic schoolroom, and the 1,900-year-old remains of buildings, alleyways and streets. Even today you can hear an underground stream, which may have formed part of ancient Rome's drainage system.

THE BASICS

basilicasanclemente.com

✚ K7

✉ Via di San Giovanni in Laterano

☎ 06 774 0021

🕐 Mon–Sat 9–12.30, 3–6, Sun excavations 12.15–6

🚇 Colosseo

🚌 C3, 3, 5, 51, 75, 87, 117, 118 to Piazza del Colosseo or 85, 117 to Via di San Giovanni in Laterano

♿ Poor

🎟 Church free; excavations moderate

HIGHLIGHTS

- The world's oldest icon of the Virgin Mary, said to be 1,000 years old, in the Pauline Chapel
- Bernini's painting *St. Cajetan Holding The Holy Child*
- The Crypt of the Nativity, with the tombs of many eminent men of the church

Santa Maria Maggiore is rightly considered Rome's finest early Christian basilica, thanks to its majestic interior and many magnificent mosaics.

History According to a myth, the Virgin appeared to Pope Liberius in his dreams on August 5, AD352, and told him to build a church exactly where snow would fall the next day. Although it was summer, snow fell, marking the outlines of a basilica on the Esquiline Hill. Legend aside, the church probably dates from AD430, though the campanile (the tallest in Rome at 75m/246ft) was added in 1377 and the interior and exterior were substantially altered in the 13th and 18th centuries. The coffered ceiling, attributed to Giuliano da Sangallo, was reputedly gilded with the first gold to arrive from the New World, a gift from Spain to Pope Alexander VI (note his Borgia bull emblems).

Rich decoration Beyond the general grandeur, the main treasures are the 36 mosaics in the architraves of the nave, fifth-century depictions of the lives of Moses, Abraham, Isaac and Jacob, framed by some 40 ancient columns. Also compelling are the mosaics in the loggia and on the triumphal arch. In the 13th-century apse are mosaics by Jacopo Torriti. Other highlights include the Cappella Sistina (tomb of Pope Sixtus V) by Domenico Fontana (1588); the Cappella Paolina, built by Paul V (1611); and Giovanni di Cosma's tomb of Cardinal Rodriguez (1299). The high altar reputedly contains a relic of Christ's crib.

THE BASICS

vatican.va

➕ K5

✉ Piazza di Santa Maria Maggiore and Piazza dell'Esquilino

☎ 06 6988 6800

🕐 Daily 7–6.45 Loggia and Museum: daily 9–6.30

Ⓜ Termini or Cavour

🚌 C3, 16, 70, 71, 75, 84, 360 to Piazza di Santa Maria Maggiore

♿ Poor: access is easiest from Piazza di Santa Maria Maggiore

💶 Church free; loggia and museum inexpensive

HIGHLIGHTS

● Plaques on the side of the building marking the height of the Tiber floods, which devastated the city between 1422 and 1870

● The church's star-spangled blue ceiling

● Relics of St. Catherine of Siena, and the preserved room in the sacristy where she died

● The headquarters of the Dominican preaching order, which serves the church, left of the building

● The sixth-century BC Egyptian obelisk above Bernini's elephant, known as Pulcino della Minerva (Minerva's chick)

Gothic Santa Maria sopra Minerva is Rome's favorite Florentine church, its plethora of frescoes, sculptures and tombs created by and commemorating the many notable Florentines who lived and worked in Rome.

Florentine influences Originally founded in the eighth century over ruins of a temple to the Roman goddess Minerva, the church was built in 1280 to a design by two Florentine Dominican monks who fashioned it on their own church, Santa Maria Novella. Before entering the church, notice its strange but charming statue of an elephant supporting an Egyptian obelisk dating from the sixth century BC in the pretty piazza outside. It was designed by Bernini in the 17th century. The elephant was chosen as an ancient symbol of piety and wisdom.

Clockwise from far left: Bernini's elephant supports an Egyptian obelisk in the piazza; the soaring Gothic arched ceiling painted blue with gold stars; the elaborate tomb of St. Catherine of Siena lies beneath the high altar; the aisles and side chapels are filled with tombs and works of art

Inside The interior of the church abounds with beautiful works, such as the Cappella Carafa (whose fine porch is attributed to Giuliano da Maiano) and Michelangelo's calm statue *The Risen Christ* (1521), left of the high altar. Filippino Lippi painted the celebrated frescoes of *St. Thomas Aquinas* and the *Assumption* (1488–93). Among other sculptures are the tombs of Francesco Tornabuoni (1480) and that of Giovanni Alberini, the latter decorated with reliefs of Hercules (15th century). Both are attributed to Mino da Fiesole. Other works include Fra Angelico's tomb slab (1455); the tombs of Medici popes Clement VII and Leo X (1536) by Antonio da Sangallo the Younger; and Bernini's monument to Maria Raggi (1643). St. Catherine of Siena, one of Italy's patron saints, is buried beneath the high altar.

THE BASICS

santamariasopraminerva.it

⊞ G5

✉ Piazza della Minerva 42

☎ 06 792 257

🕐 Mon–Fri 8–7, Sat–Sun 8–12.30, 4–7

🚌 H, 30, 40, 46, 62, 64, 70, 81, 87 to Largo di Torre Argentina

♿ Stepped access to church

🆓 Free

HIGHLIGHTS

- Cappella Costa, with the tombs of Giovanni Borgia, son of Pope Alexander VI (1492–1503), and his mother Vannozza Cattanei
- *Coronation of the Virgin*, Pinturicchio
- Cappella Cerasi, with paintings by Caravaggio and Carracci
- Fresco: *Life of San Girolamo*, Tiberio d'Assisi
- *Delphic Sybil*, Pinturicchio
- Altar, Andrea Bregno
- The oldest stained-glass windows in Rome

Santa Maria del Popolo's appeal stems from its intimate size and location, and from a wonderfully varied and rich collection of works of art ranging from masterpieces by Caravaggio to some of Rome's earliest stained-glass windows.

Renaissance achievement Founded in 1099 on the site of Nero's grave, Santa Maria del Popolo was rebuilt by Pope Sixtus IV in 1472 and extended later by Bramante and Bernini. The right nave's first chapel, the Cappella della Rovere, is decorated with frescoes on the *Life of San Girolamo* (1485–90) by Tiberio d'Assisi, a pupil of Pinturicchio whose *Nativity* (c. 1490) graces the chapel's main altar. The apse contains two fine stained-glass windows (1509) by the French artist Guillaume de Marcillat.

Clockwise from far left: Carracci's Assumption of the Virgin is the altarpiece of the Cappella Cerasi (Cerasi Chapel); Caravaggio's Crucifixion of St. Peter; the baroque facade of Santa Maria del Popolo; looking towards the richly decorated high altar

On either side are the greatest of the church's monuments: the tombs of the cardinals Ascanio Sforza (1505, left) and Girolamo Basso della Rovere (1507, right). Both are the work of Andrea Sansovino. High on the walls are superb and elegant frescoes (1508–10) of the *Virgin*, *Evangelists*, the *Fathers of the Church* and *Sybils* by Pinturicchio.

North nave The first chapel of the left transept, the Cappella Cerasi, contains three major paintings: the altarpiece, an *Assumption of the Virgin* by Annibale Carracci; and Caravaggio's dramatic *Conversion of St. Paul* and the *Crucifixion of St. Peter* (all 1601). The famous Cappella Chigi (1513), the second chapel in the north aisle, was commissioned by the Sienese banker Agostino Chigi from Raphael and Bernini.

THE BASICS

santamariadelpopolo.it

✚ F2

✉ Piazza del Popolo 12

☎ 06 361 0836

🕐 Mon–Thu 7.15–12.30, 4–7, Fri–Sat 7.30–7, Sun 7.30–1.30, 4.30–7.30

🚇 Flaminio

🚌 117 to Piazza del Popolo

♿ Few

🎟 Free

● Romanesque campanile
● Facade mosaics
● Portico
● Ceiling, by Domenichino
● Cosmati marble
pavement
● Wall tabernacle by Mino
del Reame (central nave)
● Byzantine gold mosaics
in upper and lower apse
● The nave's Roman
columns; some from the
Terme di Caracalla
● Madonna della Clemenza
in the Cappella Altemps
● Cappella Avila: baroque
chapel

TIP

● Visit in the evening, then
have a drink in one of the
outdoor cafés, from where
you can appreciate the lit
piazza and basilica.

Among the most memorable sights of
nighttime Rome are the 12th-century gold
mosaics on the facade of Santa Maria in
Trastevere, their floodlit glow casting a
gentle light over the piazza below.

Early church Santa Maria in Trastevere is
among the oldest officially sanctioned places of
worship in Rome. It was founded in around
AD222, allegedly on the spot where a fountain
of olive oil had sprung from the earth on the
day of Christ's birth (symbolizing the coming of
the grace of God). Much of the present church
was built in the 12th century during the reign of
Pope Innocent II. Inside, the main colonnade of
the nave is composed of reused and ancient
Roman columns. The portico, containing fragments of Roman reliefs and inscriptions, and

Clockwise from far left: Intricate gold mosaics adorn the upper apse; at night Santa Maria in Trastevere is bathed in light; detail of the Nativity mosaic in the upper apse; 22 columns from ancient Roman monuments divide the nave from the aisles

medieval remains, was added in 1702 by Carlo Fontana, who was responsible for the fountain that graces the adjoining piazza.

Mosaics The facade mosaics probably date from the mid-12th century, and depict the Virgin and Child with 10 lamp-carrying companions. Long believed to portray the parable of the Wise and Foolish Virgins, their subject matter is contested, as several "virgins" appear to be men and only two are carrying unlighted lamps (not the five of the parable). The mosaics of the upper apse inside the church, devoted to the glorification of the Virgin, date from the same period and are Byzantine-influenced works by Greek or Greek-trained craftsmen. Those below, depicting scenes from the life of the Virgin (1291), are by the mosaicist and fresco painter Pietro Cavallini.

THE BASICS

🔶 E7

✉ Piazza Santa Maria in Trastevere

☎ 06 581 4802

🕐 Daily 7.30am–9pm (may close 12.30–3.30 in winter)

🚌 H, 8, 780 to Viale di Trastevere, 125 to Via Manara or 23, 125, 280 to Lungotevere Raffaello Sanzio

♿ Wheelchair accessible

🆓 Free

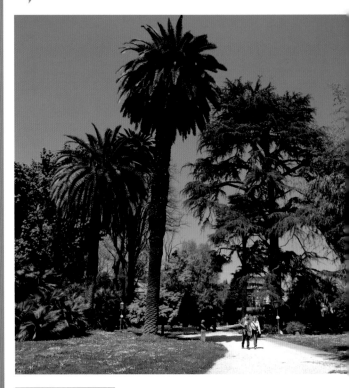

TIP

● Visit in the evening to eat
and see the facade of Santa
Maria in Trastevere floodlit.

Picturesque Trastevere gets its name from
its location "across the Tiber." Traditionally,
it was a working-class quarter, and has
long been an eating and nightlife district.
Stroll the cobbled streets, browse the quirky
stores and relax in its green spaces.

Getting your bearings Viale di Trastevere cuts
through the district, with a warren of narrow
streets running off on either side. East lies the
ancient church of Santa Cecilia in Trastevere
(▷ 73), but Trastevere's true focus is to the
west. Amble through the alleyways to Santa
Maria in Trastevere (▷ 58–59), pausing to
take in photogenic buildings and flower-draped
restaurants. Once occupied by some of Rome's
poorest families, houses here are now snapped
up by trendy urbanites, and some crumbling

Clockwise from left: A stroll in the peaceful Orto Botanico makes a refreshing break from sightseeing; view from the Orto Botanico across Rome to Villa Medici; Piazza di Santa Maria, ringed by café terraces, is a popular meeting spot

facades hide cutting-edge designer interiors. From Santa Maria, follow Via della Scala to Villa Farnesina (▷ 62–63), set below the slopes of the Gianicolo.

Botanic garden Across the main road from the Villa lies Palazzo Corsini (▷ 71), which houses an important collection of 16th- to 17th-century art, including works by Caravaggio, Rubens and Titian. Since 1883 its gardens have been home to the Orto Botanico, Rome's botanical garden, famed for its orchid houses, herb garden, trees and old roses, and a haven in the heat. It's laid out on the lower slopes of the Gianicolo, and you can head up there for fantastic views across the city. The best are from Piazzale Garibaldi, where a huge equestrian statue commemorates the hero of Italian reunification.

THE BASICS

barberinicorsini.org

✚ E8

✉ Orto Botanico, Largo Cristina di Svezia 24

☎ 06 4991 7107

🕐 Palazzo Corsini: Wed–Mon 8.30–7. Orto Botanico: Apr–Oct daily 9–6.30; Nov–Mar daily 9–5.30

🚌 H, 8, 23, 125, 280, 630, 780

♿ Few facilities

💶 Palazzo Corsini moderate (joint ticket with Palazzo Barberini). Orto Botanico inexpensive

HIGHLIGHTS

● Peruzzi's vibrant frescoes of trompe l'oeil views of Rome in the Sala delle Prospettive
● The gardens
● Raphael's fresco *Trionfo di Galatea (Triumph of Galatea)*

TIP

● Within the building is also the National Print Collection (Gabinetto Nazionale delle Stampe), part of the National Institute of Graphics, which can be visited by permission.

This is one of the most charming and intimate of all Rome's grand houses. It is known as much for its peaceful gardens as for its beautifully decorated interior, which contains works commissioned from Raphael and other artists by the villa's original owner, Agostino Chigi.

All to impress In 1508 Agostino Chigi, a wealthy banker from Siena, commissioned Baldassare Peruzzi to build him a suburban villa. Here, Chigi entertained artists, princes and cardinals. His banquets were memorable: after the meal, it is said that Chigi would have the gold and silver dishes thrown into the Tiber to impress his guests with his wealth. What they did not know was that the plates were caught by safety nets and returned to the kitchens.

Clockwise from far left: Visitors on a guided tour in the Sala delle Prospettive; the Villa Farnesina is set amid tranquil gardens; detail of a vibrant ceiling fresco by Peruzzi; Chigi's bedroom has an ornate ceiling and a fresco by Il Sodoma depicting the wedding night of Alexander the Great

In 1580, the villa was bought by the Farnese family, and it has been known as the Villa Farnesina ever since.

Lots to admire On the ground floor are the Loggia of Galatea, with a much-admired fresco by Raphael of the *Triumph of Galatea*, and the Loggia of Cupid and Psyche, frescoed according to Raphael's designs by some of his pupils (including the future star of Mannerist painting, Giulio Romano). On the upper floor is the beautiful Sala delle Prospettive, with a fresco by Baldassare Peruzzi of a trompe l'oeil colonnade through which can be seen rural landscapes, villages and a town. Finally, visit Chigi's former bedchamber, decorated with an erotic fresco, *The Wedding Night of Alexander the Great and Roxane*, by Il Sodoma.

THE BASICS

villafarnesina.it

� E6

✉ Via della Lungara 230

☎ 06 6802 7267

🕐 Daily 10–7; guided visits in English Sat and Sun 10.30

🚌 23, 125, 280 to Lungotevere della Farnesina

♿ Poor

🎫 Moderate

More to See

This section contains other great places to visit if you have more time. Some are in the heart of the city while others are a short journey away, found under Farther Afield. This chapter also has fantastic excursions that you should set aside a whole day to visit.

In the Heart of the City

ARCO DI COSTANTINO

Triumphal arches, like celebratory columns, were usually raised as monuments to military achievement, in this case the victory of Emperor Constantine over his imperial rival Maxentius in AD312. It was one of the last great monuments to be built in ancient Rome, and at 21m (69ft) high and 26m (85ft) wide it is also the largest of the city's arches. Most of its reliefs were taken from earlier buildings, partly out of pragmatism and partly out of a desire to link Constantine's glories with those of the past. The battle scenes of the central arch show Trajan at war with the Dacians; another describes a boar hunt and sacrifice to Apollo.

✚ J7 ✉ Piazza del Colosseo–Via di San Gregorio, Via dei Fori Imperiali ⏰ Daily 24 hours 🚇 Colosseo 🚌 C3, 30, 51, 75, 85, 87, 117, 118 to Piazza del Colosseo 💷 Free

AVENTINO

The southernmost of Rome's seven hills is one of the city's most beautiful quarters. Here the traffic and chaos are left far behind, replaced by peaceful churches, charming cloisters, beautiful gardens and panoramic views over Trastevere and St. Peter's.

✚ G8 🚇 Circo Massimo 🚌 C3, 3, 75, 118, 628, 673 to Via del Circo Massimo

CIRCO MASSIMO

This enormous grassy arena follows the outline of a stadium once capable of seating 300,000 people. Created to satisfy the Roman appetite for chariot racing, and the prototype for almost all subsequent racecourses, it was begun around 326BC and modified frequently before the occasion of its last recorded use in AD549. Much of the original structure was robbed of its stone—old monuments were often ransacked for building materials—but the circuit's dividing wall remains, along with the ruins of the imperial box and the open arena, now a public park. Avoid after dark.

✚ H8 ✉ Via del Circo Massimo ⏰ Daily 24 hours 🚇 Circo Massimo 🚌 C3, 75, 81, 118, 160, 628, 673 to Piazza di Porta Capena 💷 Free

The Arco di Costantino

COLONNA DI MARCO AURELIO

The Column of Marcus Aurelius (AD180–96) celebrates Aurelius's military triumphs over hostile north European tribes. It is composed of 27 separate drums of Carrara marble molded into a seamless whole, and is decorated with a continuous spiral of bas-reliefs commemorating episodes from the victorious campaigns. Aurelius is depicted no fewer than 59 times, though curiously never actually in battle. At the top of the 50m (140ft) structure stands a statue of St. Paul, which replaced the 60th depiction of Aurelius in 1589.

🔁 G5 ⊠ Piazza Colonna, Via del Corso ⏰ Daily 24 hours 🚇 Barberini 🚌 62, 63, 85, 95, 117 and all routes to Via del Corso ✋ Free

CRYPTA BALBI

coopculture.it

This museum, part of the Museo Nazionale Romano, contains the ruins of a theater built in 13BC, along with a collection of objects to illustrate social, economic and urban planning changes from ancient times through the Middle Ages to the present day. Two other sections have displays of vases, glassware, mosaics and other items dating from between the fifth and eighth centuries.

🔁 G6 ⊠ Via delle Botteghe Oscure 31 ⏰ 06 3996 7701; book online at coopculture.it ⏰ Tue–Sun 9–7.45 🚇 Colosseo 🚌 30, 40, 46, 62, 64, 70, 81, 87, 130, 190 to Largo di Torre Argentina ✋ Moderate (combined ticket)

LE DOMUS ROMANE

palazzovalentini.it

The Palazzo Valentini, a municipal office building, stands on top of the remains of some extremely upscale third-century AD Roman houses. These have been excavated and brought to life using every type of modern technology, giving visitors a genuine taste of prosperous life in upper-class ancient Rome. Tours take you into the houses where, through a glass floor, you see the ruins springing back to life, as frescoes

St. Paul atop the Colonna di Marco Aurelio

Fontana del Tritone, Piazza Barberini

miraculously reappear on walls, floors are laid with mosaics, and sounds and light evoke the past. It makes a wonderful introduction to the city's ruins.

🚌 H6 ✉ Palazzo Valentini, Via Foro Traiano 85 ☎ 06 2276 1280 (info and tel booking) 🕐 Daily 9.30–6.30 🚌 60, 62, 64, 85, 492 and all services to Piazza Venezia 💶 Expensive ❓ Tickets can't be bought at the Palazzo. Either call for tickets or book online at tosc.it

FONTANA DELLE TARTARUGHE
This tiny gem of a fountain (1581–84) is one of Rome's most delightful, thanks to the four turtles, probably added by Bernini in 1658 (the current bronze sculptures are copies).

🚌 F6 ✉ Piazza Mattei 🚌 H, 8, 63, 780 to Via Arenula or 30, 70, 87 and other services to Largo di Torre Argentina

FONTANA DEL TRITONE
Like its companion piece, the Fontana delle Api, the Fontana del Tritone (1643) was also designed by Bernini for Urban VIII. One of the sculptor's earliest fountains, the Fountain of the Triton depicts four dolphins supporting twin scallop shells bearing the Barberini coat of arms, on which the triumphant Triton is enthroned.

🚌 H4 ✉ Piazza Barberini 🚇 Barberini 🚌 C3, 53, 62, 63, 71, 80, 83, 85, 160, 492 to Piazza Barberini or Via del Tritone

FORI IMPERIALI
All five of the Imperial Fora that are featured in the Museo dei Fori Imperiali (▷ 29) stretch between the museum area and the Colosseum, and it's worth the walk to see them all. Built as political and commercial hubs by successive emperors, they have been ruthlessly plundered over time, and may seem like a haphazard collection of columns and tumbled stone, but seeing them close up is still fascinating. Excavations are ongoing and what has been unearthed represents only half of the original fora.

🚌 H6 ✉ Via dei Fori Imperiali ☎ 06 679 7702 or 06 0608 🕐 Visible from outside only 🚇 Colosseo 🚌 51, 75, 85, 87, 117, 118 to Via dei Fori Imperiali 💶 Free

The ruins of the Temple of Minerva, Fori Imperiali

Synagogue in the Ghetto quarter

GHETTO

museoebraico.roma.it

This picturesque place, its narrow streets full of Jewish restaurants, pastry shops and workshops, is still a meeting place for the Romano-Jewish community. The 1904 synagogue, overlooking the Tiber, houses the Jewish Museum, its dome visible from much of the city.

➕ F6 ✉ Museo: Via Catalana (Largo 16 Ottobre 1943) ☎ 06 6840 0661 🕐 Apr–Sep Sun–Thu 10–6 (last admission 5.15), Fri 10–4 (last admission 3.15); Oct–Mar Sun–Thu 10–5 (last admission 4.15), Fri 10–2 (last admission 1.15) 🚌 H, 23, 28, 63 to Lungotevere Pierleoni 🎫 Moderate (includes tour of synagogue)

ISOLA TIBERINA

This small island in the Tiber, with its medieval buildings and Roman bridges, feels like a safe haven, protected from the chaos of the city. The island is on a volcanic rock and its shape resembles that of a ship. Two bridges join it to the riverbanks: the Ponte Cestio dates back to the first century BC, and leads to Trastevere; while the Ponte Fabricio, built in 62BC, the only Roman bridge to survive intact, joins the island to the Ghetto.

➕ F7 🚌 H, 23, 63, 280, 780 to Lungotevere dei Cenci and all services to Via Arenula and Largo di Torre Argentina

MACRO

museomacro.org

Opened in 1999, this modern museum is housed in a converted brewery, with a stunning extension designed by Odile Decq. It showcases contemporary Italian art from the 1950s onward and provides space for large-scale site-specific works and installations created by young artists.

➕ L2 ✉ Via Nizza 138 ☎ 06 696 271 🕐 Tue–Fri, Sun 10–8, Sat 10–10 🚌 38, 90 🎫 Expensive

MONTE PALATINO

After a stroll around the Forum it's worth climbing the Palatine Hill to enjoy this peaceful spot. Orange groves, cypresses and drowsy corners, all speckled with flowers and ancient stones, make up the Orti Farnesiani (Farnesian Gardens),

The Basilica di San Bartolomeo all'Isola, Isola Tiberina

which were laid out in the 16th century over the ruins of the palace that once stood here.

🔲 H7 ✉ Entrances from Via di San Gregorio 30 and other entrances to Roman Forum ☎ 06 3996 7700 🕓 Hours as for Colosseo (▷ 19) 🚇 Colosseo 🚌 75, 87, 117 to Via dei Fori Imperiali 🎫 Expensive (joint ticket valid for two days with Colosseo and Foro Romano)

MUSEO DELL'ARA PACIS

arapacis.it

Augustus's Altar of Peace, now contained within architect Richard Meier's controversial glass pavilion (opened in 2006), is decorated with bas-reliefs from 9BC. It was built to celebrate Augustus's triumphal return to Rome after campaigns in Spain and Gaul, and to commemorate the peace he had established throughout the Roman world. The outside of the enclosure is decorated with mythological scenes and grand processional friezes in which life-size figures portray Augustus, the imperial family, officials and other notables.

🔲 F4 ✉ Lungotevere in Augusta, at the corner of Via Tomacelli ☎ 06 60608; book online at ticket.museiincomuneroma.it 🕓 Daily 9.30–7.30 🚇 Spagna 🚌 C3, 301, 628 to Piazza Augusto Imperatore or 301, 628 to Lungotevere in Augusta 🎫 Moderate

MUSEO KEATS-SHELLEY

keats-shelley-house.org

Since 1909 the final home of Keats, where he died in 1821 at the age of 25, has been a museum and library for students of the Romantic poets Keats and Shelley. Books, pictures and essays lie scattered around the house.

🔲 G4 ✉ Piazza di Spagna 26 ☎ 06 678 4235 🕓 Mon–Sat 10–1, 2–6 🚇 Spagna 🚌 117 to Piazza di Spagna 🎫 Inexpensive

MUSEO NAZIONALE ETRUSCO DI VILLA GIULIA

museoetru.it

The most important collection of Etruscan art and objects in the world is housed in a beautiful 16th-century villa built by Pope Julius III. Exhibits from sites in west central and southern Italy include

A 15th-century painting, Museo Nazionale del Palazzo di Venezia

The loggia of the Villa Giulia

Greek vases, jewelry, giant figures and tomb relics. The collection is huge, so be selective in choosing what to see.

🔲 G1 ✉ Piazzale di Villa Giulia 9 ☎ 06 322 6571; book online at tosc.it 🕐 Tue–Sun 8.30–7.30 🚋 2, 19 💶 Moderate

MUSEO NAZIONALE DEL PALAZZO DI VENEZIA

museopalazzovenezia.beniculturali.it
Built in 1455 for Pietro Barbo (later Pope Paul II), the former Venetian Embassy became the property of the state in 1916. There are temporary exhibitions and a permanent collection including Renaissance paintings, sculpture, armor and silverware.

🔲 G6 ✉ Palazzo Venezia, Via del Plebiscito 118 ☎ 06 678 0131, 06 6999 4284 🕐 Tue–Sun 8.30–7.30 🚋 All services to Piazza Venezia 💶 Moderate (inexpensive during exhibitions)

PALAZZO CORSINI

barberinicorsini.org
Though in a separate building, this gallery is part of the Palazzo Barberini's Galleria Nazionale.

Originally part of the Corsini family's 17th-century collection, it became the property of the state in 1883. Pictures from the 16th to 18th centuries hang alongside bronzes and sculptures in elegant rooms.

🔲 E6 ✉ Via della Lungara 10 ☎ 06 6880 2323, reservations 06 328 10; book online at tosc.it 🕐 Wed–Mon 8.30–7 🚋 23, 280, 870 to Lungotevere della Farnesina 💶 Moderate

PALAZZO SPADA

galleriaspada.beniculturali.it
This pretty palazzo, with a creamy stucco facade (1556–62), has four rooms where you can admire the 17th- and 18th-century Spada family paintings. Cardinal Bernardino Spada is portrayed by Guido Reni; there's a fine Borromini *Perspective* and works by Albrecht Dürer, Andrea del Sarto and others.

🔲 F6 ✉ Piazza Capo di Ferro 13–Vicolo del Polverone 15b ☎ 06 328 10; book online at ticketone.it 🕐 Wed–Mon 8.30–7.30 🚋 H, 8, 63, 780 to Via Arenula 💶 Inexpensive

The entrance to Palazzo Corsini

A replica gilded bronze statue of Marcus Aurelius in the center of Piazza del Campidoglio

PIAZZA DEL CAMPIDOGLIO

This piazza, one of Rome's most beautiful squares, was designed by Michelangelo on the Capitoline Hill, for Emperor Charles V's triumphal entry into Rome in 1536. The buildings that stand on three sides of the square—the Palazzo Senatorio, the Palazzo Nuovo and the Palazzo dei Conservatori—were part of his scheme.

➕ G6 ✉ Piazza del Campidoglio 🚇 Colosseo 🚌 Services to Piazza Venezia

PINCIO

The park was laid out in the early 19th century. Walk to the Pincio from Piazza del Popolo or Piazza di Spagna to enjoy wonderful views (best at dusk) across the rooftops to St. Peter's.

➕ G2 ✉ Piazza del Pincio 🕐 Daily dawn–dusk 🚌 117 to Piazzale Flaminio or Piazza del Popolo 🎫 Free

SAN GIOVANNI IN LATERANO

vatican.va

Until the 14th century, when the popes moved to the Vatican, San Giovanni was the pontiff's seat.

When the fourth-century original was rebuilt in the 17th century after barbarians, earthquakes and fires destroyed it, it was modeled on St. Peter's.

➕ L8 ✉ Piazza San Giovanni in Laterano ☎ 06 6988 6433 🕐 Church Apr–Sep daily 7–7; Oct–Mar 7–6/6.30. Cloisters daily 9–6; Oct–Mar 9–5. Baptistry daily 7.30–12.30, 4–6 🚇 San Giovanni 🚌 85, 117 to Piazza San Giovanni 🎫 Church free; cloisters and baptistry inexpensive

SAN LUIGI DEI FRANCESI

saint-louis-rome.net

The church of the French community in Rome was built between 1518 and 1589 and is devoted to St. Louis (Louis XI of France). Its Renaissance facade conceals three late masterpieces (1597–1602) by Caravaggio, all depicting episodes from the life of St. Matthew: his *Calling*, *Martyrdom* and *Inspiration*.

➕ F5 ✉ Piazza di San Luigi dei Francesi 5 ☎ 06 688 271 🕐 Mon–Fri 9.30–12.45, 2.30–6.30, Sat 9.30–12.15, 2.30–6.30, Sun 11.30–12.45, 2.30–6.30 🚌 30, 70, 81, 87, 130, 492 to Corso del Rinascimento 🎫 Free

Inside San Giovanni in Laterano

Caravaggio's Inspiration of St. Matthew, *San Luigi dei Francesi*

SAN PIETRO IN VINCOLI

Rebuilt in 1475 over a basilica founded in 440, the church takes its name from the chains *(vincoli)* kept in a coffer under the high altar. It is said they are the chains used to bind St. Peter while he was held in the Mamertine prison.

➕ J6 ✉ Piazza di San Pietro in Vincoli 4a ☎ 06 9784 4950 🕐 Daily 8–12/12.30, 3.30–7 (Oct–Mar 3–6) 🚇 Colosseo or Cavour 🚌 75, 117 to Via Cavour or C3, 3, 51, 75, 85, 87, 117, 175 to Piazza del Colosseo 💷 Free

SANTA CECILIA IN TRASTEVERE

benedettinesantacecilia.it

This church is devoted to Cecilia, a young Roman woman who was martyred in the third century AD. Enter through a courtyard, with a portico supported by old granite columns and a lily garden with a central fountain. Next you pass a facade designed by Ferdinando Fuga in 1741. Crypt excavations and splendid ninth-century apse mosaics depicting Jesus with saints Paul, Agatha, Peter, Paschal,

Valerian and Cecilia are among Santa Cecilia's treasures. Another is the fresco *Last Judgment* (1293) by Pietro Cavallini, the remains of a medieval masterpiece.

➕ F8 ✉ Piazza di Santa Cecilia 22 ☎ 06 589 9289 or 06 581 2140 🕐 Mon–Sat 10–12.30, 4–6, Sun 11.30–12.30, 4–6. Cavallini frescoes Mon–Sat 10–12.30. Crypt/excavations daily 10–1, 4–7 🚌 H, 8, 23, 780 to Viale di Trastevere or Lungotevere Ripa 💷 Church free; Cavallini fresco inexpensive; crypt inexpensive

SANTA MARIA IN ARACOELI

Perched atop the Capitoline Hill, Santa Maria in Aracoeli, with its glorious ceiling, fine frescoes and soft chandelier-lit interior, is a calm retreat from the ferocious traffic of Piazza Venezia just outside. The flight of 124 steep steps approaching Santa Maria was built in 1348 to celebrate either the end of a plague epidemic or the Holy Year proclaimed for 1350. The church is first recorded in AD574, but even then it was old. Most of the present structure, however, dates from 1260.

Stefano Maderno's altar sculpture of St. Cecilia in Santa Cecilia in Trastevere (1599–1600)

Fresco of St. Benedict, Santa Maria in Aracoeli

⊞ G6 ✉ Piazza d'Aracoeli ☎ 06 6976 3839 🕒 May–Sep daily 9–6.30; Oct–Apr 9.30–5.30 🚌 40, 46, 62, 64, 70, 80 and all other services to Piazza Venezia 🎟 Free

SANTA MARIA DELLA CONCEZIONE

cappucciniviaveneto.it

Lying in the crypt of Santa Maria della Concezione, built in 1624, are the remains of 4,000 Capuchin monks, some still dressed, the bones of others crafted into bizarre chandeliers and wall decorations. The bodies were originally buried in soil especially imported from Jerusalem. When this ran out they were left uncovered, a practice that continued until 1870.

⊞ H4 ✉ Via Vittorio Veneto 27 ☎ 06 8880 3695 🕒 Church Mon–Sat 7–1, 3–6, Sun 9.30–12, 3.30–6. Crypt (Cimitero dei Cappuccini) daily 9–7 🚇 Barberini–Fontana Trevi 🚌 C3, 53, 61, 63, 80, 83 to Via Vittorio Veneto 🎟 Moderate

SANTA MARIA IN COSMEDIN

This lovely medieval church is best known for the Bocca della Verità (Mouth of Truth) in the portico.

This weather-beaten marble face of the sea god Oceanus was once used by the ancient Romans as a drain cover. Legend claims that the mouth will clamp shut on the hands of liars. Inside, the church has a beautiful floor, twin pulpits, a bishop's throne and a stone choir screen, all in fine Cosmati stone inlay. Most of these date from the 12th century, while the *baldacchino* (altar canopy) was built by Deodato di Cosma in 1294. In a room off the right aisle is a mosaic depicting the *Adoration of the Magi*, almost all that remains of an eighth-century Greek church on the site.

⊞ G7 ✉ Piazza della Bocca della Verità 18 ☎ 06 678 7759 🕒 Apr–Oct daily 9.30–6; Nov–Mar 9.30–5 🚌 C3, 23, 81, 116, 118, 280 and other routes to Piazza Bocca della Verità or Lungotevere Pierleoni 🎟 Free

TEMPIO DI VESTA AND TEMPIO DELLA FORTUNA VIRILIS

The Tempio di Vesta and Tempio della Fortuna Virilis are the two best-preserved ancient temples

Temple of Fortuna Virilis

The Bocca della Verità, Santa Maria in Cosmedin

in Rome—all but one of the 20 columns of the former remain standing. Both date from the second century BC, the first named after its resemblance to a similar temple in the Roman Forum. The origins of the second, and the god Portunus to whom it was dedicated, remain a mystery.

🚇 G7 ✉ Piazza Bocca della Verità 7 🚌 C3, H, 30, 44, 63, 80, 83, 118 and other services to Via del Teatro del Marcello and Piazza Bocca della Verità

TRIUMPHS AND LAMENTS

Created by South African artist William Kentridge in 2016, this stunning monumental frieze, 550m (600yds) long and 10m (33ft) high, stretches along the Tiber embankment walls mirroring horizontally the scenes unfolding on a triumphal column. It's a procession of 80 images, a series of symbols, archetypes and events that tell the artist's version of Rome's history.

🚇 E6 ✉ Lungotevere della Farnesina ⏰ Always visible 🚌 23, 125, 280 to Lungotevere della Farnesina 🖐 Free

VILLA BORGHESE

Rome's largest central park was laid out between 1613 and 1616 as the grounds of the Borghese family's summer villa. This shady retreat has walkways, woods and lakes that are complemented by an array of statues, temples and fountains, a racetrack, playgrounds and the Bioparco—a zoo and ecological center ideal for those traveling with children.

🚇 H2 ✉ Porta Pinciana–Via Flaminia ☎ Bioparco 06 360 8211; bioparco.it ⏰ Daily dawn–dusk; Bioparco Apr–Oct daily 9.30–6; Nov–Mar 9.30–5 🚇 Flaminio 🚌 3, 19, 52, 53, 217, 360, 495, 910 🖐 Free; Bioparco very expensive

VILLA CELIMONTANA

Set on one of the southern hills of ancient Rome and scattered with the remains of ancient buildings, this is one of the city's lesser-known parks. It is easily accessible from the Colosseum and San Giovanni in Laterano.

🚇 J8 ✉ Piazza della Navicella ⏰ Daily 7–dusk 🚌 3 to Via del Parco del Celio or 117, 673 to Via Claudia 🖐 Free

The Temple of Diana in the leafy park of Villa Borghese

Farther Afield

CATACOMBE DI SAN CALLISTO

catacombe.roma.it

These second-century catacombs are the largest and most impressive in Rome—and the most popular. They extend over 20km (12 miles) on five levels, with over 170,000 Christian burial places. You can explore claustrophobic tunnels and *loculi*, or burial niches, carved from the soft tufa stone.

🔲 See map ▷ 115 ✉ Via Appia Antica 110/126 ☎ 06 513 0151 🕐 Thu–Tue 9–12, 2–5; closed Feb 🚌 714 to Piazza di San Giovanni in Laterano, then bus 218 to Fosse Ardeatine 💶 Inexpensive

CATACOMBE DI SAN SEBASTIANO

catacombe.org

Above the catacombs is the fourth-century basilica, dedicated to St. Sebastian, martyred by arrows, who was buried on this spot in the third century. The catacombs themselves were among the most important burial places in early Christian Rome, and may even have housed the bodies of saints Peter and Paul.

🔲 See map ▷ 115 ✉ Via Appia Antica 136 ☎ 06 785 0350 🕐 Mon–Sat 10–5 (last admission 4.30); closed Dec 🚇 Line B to Colosseo or Circo Massimo then bus 118; line A to San Giovanni then bus 218 💶 Inexpensive

MAXXI

maxxi.art

The Museo Nazionale delle Arti del XXI Secolo, an extraordinary gallery of 21st-century art, includes work from the last 40 years as well as cutting-edge contemporary Italian and international art.

🔲 See map ▷ 114 ✉ Via Guido Reni 4a ☎ 06 320 1954 🕐 Tue–Fri, Sun 11–7, Sat 11–10 🚇 Line A to Flaminio then tram 2 🚌 53, 168, 280, 910 💶 Moderate; free to Gallery 4 Tue–Fri and last Sun of month

MONTE GIANICOLO

The best view of Rome is from the Janiculum Hill. There are views all the way up from the Passeggiata del Gianicolo, an avenue that runs around the hill. En route visit the little Tempietto designed by Bramante in 1508, and the church of San Pietro in Montorio.

The view from the Gianicolo

Zaha Hadid's remarkable MAXXI gallery of modern art

D7 ⊠ Passeggiata del Gianicolo
Tempietto Via Garibaldi 33: Tue–Sun
10–6; church daily 8–12, 3–4 115, 125,
870 to the Gianicolo or Via Garibaldi
Church and Tempietto free

SAN PAOLO FUORI LE MURA
basilicasanpaolo.org

The church of St. Paul outside
the Walls marks the spot where
St. Paul was buried after his death
in AD67. Begun in AD385, it
replaced several smaller churches
on the site. It was one of the city's
most richly decorated buildings,
but a fire in 1823 destroyed the
church and most of its treasures.

Much of the vast church you
see today dates from the 19th
century, though one or two artistic
masterpieces survived the fire,
notably a beautiful altar canopy by
the artist Arnolfo di Cambio dating
from 1285.

See map ▷ 114 ⊠ Piazzale San
Paolo 1, Via Ostiense 186 06 6988
0800/0802 Daily 7–6.30 (5.30 in winter)
Line B to Basilica di San Paolo 23 to
Ostiense/LGT San Paolo or 271 to Viale di
San Paolo Free

TERME DI CARACALLA
coopculture.it

Ancient Rome's luxurious baths
could hold as many as 1,600
bathers. Started by Septimius
Severus in AD206, and completed
11 years later by his son, Caracalla,
they were designed for gatherings
as well as for hygiene. The site is
now a venue for outdoor opera
and concerts.

J9 ⊠ Via delle Terme di Caracalla 52
06 3996 7702; book online at
coopculture.it Tue–Sun 9–1 hour before
sunset, Mon 8.30–2; closed public holidays
Circo Massimo C3, 75, 81, 118, 160,
628, 760 to Via di San Gregorio–Via delle
Terme di Caracalla Moderate (combined
L'Archaeologia card gives admission to
tombs on Via Appia)

VILLA DORIA PAMPHILJ

If you fancy a long walk away from
the crowds, there's nowhere better
than here in Rome's largest public
landscaped park. Jogging and
cycling are popular activities.

B8 ⊠ Via di San Pancrazio Daily
dawn–dusk 115, 125, 870 to the
Gianicolo or Via Garibaldi

San Paolo Fuori le Mura's apse mosaic,
depicting Christ flanked by the Apostles

Ancient Rome's public baths, Terme di Caracalla

Excursions

FRASCATI

Frascati is the loveliest of the Castelli Romani, 13 towns in the Colli Albani, south of Rome, so-called because they grew up around the feudal castles of the city's popes and patrician families. The Colli Albani are 60km (37 miles) of volcanic hills, known for their wine, lakes, pretty countryside and—above all—as a refuge from the summer heat of Rome.

Many of the Castelli were badly damaged during fighting in 1944 and have a number of modern buildings. Frascati, however, retains much of its charm, and is also the easiest town to reach from central Rome. Come by train and you are rewarded with an appealing ride through some of the Roman Campagna (countryside) as the line climbs into the hills.

The chances are that if you drink house white wine in Rome's restaurants it will come from Frascati, or near by, but the locals say it is best drunk *sul posto* (on the spot). There are any number of cafés and *fraschette* (taverns)

dotted around the pedestrian-only old quarter—one of the most historic is the Grappolo d'Oro at Piazza Fabio Filzi 5; or visit the stalls in Piazza del Mercato.

The grandest of Frascati's villas is the Villa Aldobrandini, above Piazza Marconi. It was designed in 1598 by Giacomo della Porta for Cardinal Pietro Aldobrandini, a nephew of Pope Clement VII. The great villa itself, all faded majesty, is rarely open, but visits are generally possible to the wonderful baroque garden. Don't miss the sweeping views from the main front terrace.

Elsewhere, visit the cathedral, the church of Il Gesù, and the town park, formerly the gardens of the Villa Torlonia, which was destroyed in 1944.

Distance: 20km (12 miles)
Journey time: 30–40 min
🚆 Train from Termini 🚌 COTRAL bus from Anagnina metro station
Villa Aldobrandini
✉ Via Cardinale Massaia 18 ☎ 06 683 3785 🕐 Garden only Mon–Sat 9–5
🎫 Free

Views of the countryside around Frascati
The terraces at Villa Aldobrandini are decorated with statues

TIVOLI

Tivoli is one of the most popular excursions from Rome, thanks to the town's lovely wooded position on a bend of the River Aniene, the superlative gardens of the Villa d'Este and the ruins and grounds of Hadrian's Roman villa. It can be busy, especially at weekends, so arrive early to see everything.

The Este gardens were laid out in 1550 as part of a country retreat for Cardinal Ippolito d'Este, son of Lucrezia Borgia and the Duke of Ferrara. Highlights among the terraces and fountains are the Fontana dell'Organo (Organ Fountain), which plays tunes, and the Fontana della Civetta (Owl Fountain), which spouts birdsong.

Also worth seeing is the Villa Gregoriana, a more unkempt park created in 1831. Explore the paths through the park's gorge for some fine views of the luxuriant vegetation and two crashing waterfalls.

The Villa Adriana requires a trip out of town but it is well worth it for its romantic classical ruins. The largest villa discovered in the Roman Empire, it was built between AD118 and AD135 as a retirement home for Emperor Hadrian and covered an area greater than the center of Rome.

Distance: 31km (19 miles)

Journey time: 1 hour

🚆 Train from Termini 🚇 Metro line B to Ponte Mammolo and then COTRAL bus to Tivoli in direction Via Prenestina

Villa d'Este

villadestetivoli.info

✉ Piazza Trento ☎ 199 766 166; book online at vivaticket.it ⏰ Tue–Sun 8.30–1 hour before dusk; last admission 90 min before closing 🎟 Moderate

Villa Gregoriana

visitfai.it/parcovillagregoriana

✉ Piazza Tempio di Vesta and Largo Sant' Angelo ☎ 0774 332650 ⏰ Apr–Oct daily 10–6.30; Mar, mid-Nov to mid-Dec Tue–Sun 10–4 (closed mid-Dec to Feb) 🎟 Moderate

Villa Adriana

villaadriana.beniculturali.it

✉ Via di Villa Adriana–Via Tiburtina ☎ 06 3996 7900; book online at coopculture.it ⏰ Daily 9–1 hour before dusk 🚌 CAT shuttle bus 4 or 4X from Tivoli center 🎟 Moderate

The Organ Fountain in the grounds of the Villa d'Este

City Tours

This section contains self-guided tours that will help you explore the sights in each of the city's regions. Each tour is designed to take a day, with a map pinpointing the recommended places along the way. There is a quick reference guide at the end of each tour, listing everything you need in that region, so you know exactly what's close by.

CITY TOURS

The Ancient City

Ancient monuments can be found across present-day Rome, but the heart of the ancient city centers on an area containing the Roman Forum, the Colosseum and several other majestic ruins, along with magnificent churches and grand museums.

Morning
Start your day in **Piazza Venezia** and admire the **Monumento a Vittorio Emanuele II**, the vast white edifice that dominates this big and busy square. Then climb the ramp, designed by Michelangelo, to **Piazza del Campidoglio** (▷ 72) and pay a quick visit to **Santa Maria in Aracoeli** (▷ 73–74). Exit the piazza down the lane in its far left corner for a lovely overview of the Roman Forum before descending to Via dei Fori Imperiali to look at the **Fori Imperiali** (▷ 68), located below street level either side of the road. Then allow a good hour or two to explore the **Foro Romano** itself (▷ 22–23).

Mid-morning
The Forum has little shade, so toward the end of your visit climb the slopes of **Monte Palatino** (▷ 69–70) for a break in its shady gardens. Your Forum ticket is valid for the Palatine and for the **Colosseo** (▷ 18–19), which you should visit next—exit the Forum beyond the Arco di Tito and the amphitheater is in front of you. Don't overlook the **Arco di Costantino** (▷ 66), on your right just after you exit the Forum, and be sure to join the correct ticket-holders' line for the Colosseum.

Lunch
Check your watch and, if it's still open, visit **San Pietro in Vincoli** (left; ▷ 73), barely five minutes' walk from the Colosseum. For lunch, avoid the generally poor-quality cafés in Piazza del Colosseo and walk a few minutes to one of the evening choices (see facing page). Alternatively, you can eat a picnic in the nearby **Parco di Traiano**.

Afternoon

If you like churches, now is the time to visit **San Giovanni in Laterano** (▷ 72), which is open all day. If you want less of a walk, and a more manageable and fascinating church, restrict yourself to **San Clemente** (right; ▷ 50–51), but note that it does not usually open until mid-afternoon.

Mid-afternoon

Retrace your steps to Piazza del Campidoglio and perhaps take a break on the terrace café of the Monumento a Vittorio Emanuele II, which has good views of the **Fori Imperiali** (▷ 68). If you still have the energy for a museum, see the **Musei Capitolini** (▷ 24–25). If the **Mercati di Traiano** (▷ 28–29) or **Le Domus Romane** (▷ 67–68) sound more appealing, they are both within a short walk of Piazza Venezia, just down the steps from the Capitoline.

Evening

It is well worth returning here at night, or remaining here at the end of your day, to enjoy the sight of several floodlit monuments, especially the **Colosseo** (left; ▷ 18–19) and **Piazza del Campidoglio** (▷ 72). Climb the steps or take the escalator to the terrace (Largo G. Agnesi) above the Colosseo metro station for an especially good view of the amphitheater. If it's early and you just want a snack or light meal, try the **Oppio Caffè** (▷ 135) in the Parco di Traiano; for a fuller meal, the grid of streets east of the Colosseum has several choices, including **Pasqualino** (▷ 149) and **Il Bocconcino** (▷ 143), which both serve good food.

Via della Dataria
Palazzo del Quirinale
Piazza del Quirinale
Palazzo delle Esposizioni

5
Palazzo Sciarra
Sant'Ignazio di Loyola
Palazzo-Galleria Doria Pamphilj
Palazzo Odescalchi
Santi Apostoli
Piazza dei Santi Apostoli
Palazzo Colonna
Villa Colonna

Palazzo Altieri
Museo Nazionale del Palazzo di Venezia
Chiesa del Gesù
San Marco
Piazza Venezia
Le Domus Romane
Colonna Traiana
Largo Magnanapoli

Via Panisperna

Museo dei Fori Imperiali e Mercati di Traiano

6
Piazza Venezia
Monumento a Vittorio Emanuele II
Fori Imperiali
Santa Maria in Aracoeli
Piazza del Campidoglio

Cavour 313

San Pietro in Vincoli

Piazza del Campitelli
Musei Capitolini
Monte Capitolino
Arco di Settimio Severo
Santi Cosma e Damiano

Teatro di Marcello
Piazza Monte Savello
Santa Nicola in Carcere
Foro Romano
Arco di Tito
Colosseo

7
Tempio della Fortuna Virilis
Tempio di Vesta
Piazza di S Anastasia
S Teodoro
Orti Farnesiani
Monte Palatino
Colosseo
Arco di Costantino

Piazza Bocca della Verità
Santa Maria in Cosmedin
Sant'Anastasia
Casa di Livia
Palazzo dei Flavi
Domus Augusti
Cavour 313
Tempio del Divo Claudio
Parco del Celio

Tevere
S Vincenzo de Paoli
AVENTINO
Circo Massimo
Basilica Santi Giovanni e Paolo
San Gregorio Magno

8
Piazzale Ugo La Malfa
Circo Maximo Experience
Piazza di Porta Capena
Obelisco di Axum
Circo Massimo

S Prisca
Piazza Tempio Diana
Albania
Stadio delle Terme di Caracalla

9
Aventino (Albania)
Santa Balbina
Parco di Porta Capena

0 — 500 m
0 — 500 yds

G   H   J

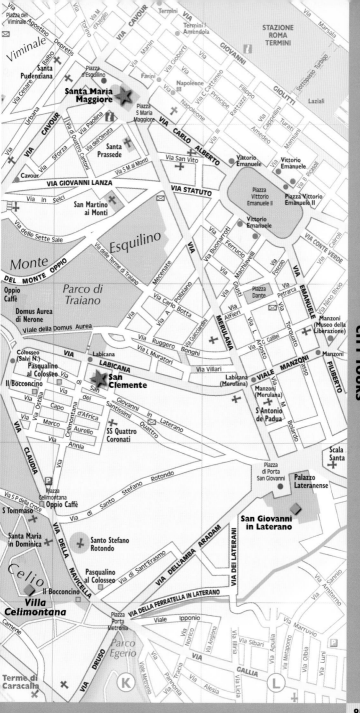

The Ancient City Quick Reference Guide

 SIGHTS AND EXPERIENCES

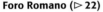

Colosseo (▷ 18)

The Colosseum is the greatest surviving monument from Roman antiquity, a huge amphitheater built in the first century AD to stage gladiatorial combats and games.

Foro Romano (▷ 22)

Ruins in the Roman Forum span almost 1,500 years, the legacy of an era when this was the political, social, religious and administrative hub of the Roman Empire.

Musei Capitolini (▷ 24)

These two museums on the Capitoline Hill contain Roman and Greek masterpieces, as well as an outstanding collection of Renaissance and other paintings.

Museo dei Fori Imperiali e Mercati di Traiano (▷ 28)

Once the Foro Romano became too cramped, successive emperors created new imperial fora, including Trajan's market complex.

San Clemente (▷ 50)

Three places of worship make up this multi-level complex: a medieval church, an earlier church below and an ancient Roman Mithraic temple below that.

Santa Maria Maggiore (▷ 52)

This fourth-century basilica is one of the great churches of Rome, its vast interior graced with lavishly decorated chapels, and fifth-century mosaics in the nave.

Central Rome

Central Rome embraces the medieval, Renaissance and baroque heart of the city, offering a superb variety of palaces, churches, galleries, shops, markets, restaurants and cafés, cobbled streets and fountain-filled piazzas.

Morning
Join the market traders early for a cappuccino in **Piazza Campo de' Fiori** (▷ 44–45), being sure to walk into the adjoining **Piazza Farnese** to admire its fountains and the **Palazzo Farnese**. If the small **Palazzo Spada** gallery (▷ 71) appeals, now is the time to see it. Then make your way to the **Pantheon** (right; ▷ 42–43) via Largo di Torre Argentina, Via dei Cestari (known for shops selling ecclesiastical wear) and **Santa Maria sopra Minerva** (▷ 54–55). From the Pantheon walk to **Piazza Navona** (▷ 46–47) via **San Luigi dei Francesi** (▷ 72), with its dramatic late master-pieces by Caravaggio, and then along Corso del Rinascimento.

Mid-morning
Cafés on and around Piazza Navona are often expensive, especially if you sit outside, but it's worth paying over the odds to enjoy the lovely setting. Away from the square, **Bar del Fico** (▷ 143) is a local favorite. So, too, are **La Tazza d'Oro** (▷ 151) and **Sant'Eustachio** (▷ 150) nearer the Pantheon, not so much for their setting but because both claim to offer Rome's best cup of coffee.

Lunch
Before lunch, devote an hour or so to exploring the pretty streets west of **Piazza Navona** (left), many of which contain interesting shops and plenty of options for a light lunch. Via del Governo Vecchio, Via dei Coronari and Via dei Banchi Nuovi are especially good, as are Via dei Banchi Vecchi, Via Giulia and Via dei Cappellari west of Piazza Campo de' Fiori.

CITY TOURS

Afternoon

The afternoon can be devoted to two galleries, with relatively small but superb collections of contrasting exhibits: the Roman sculptures of the **Palazzo Altemps** (▷ 34–35), which is open all day and is a short walk north of Piazza Navona, and the paintings of the **Palazzo-Galleria Doria Pamphilj** (▷ 38–39). Walk between the two via Piazza di Montecitorio and the **Colonna di Marco Aurelio** (▷ 67).

Evening

The area around **Piazza Navona** (right) is one of the city's main restaurant districts, so there are plenty of options (not all good) in the narrow, medieval streets, many of which are lined with tables spilling onto the cobbles on summer evenings. Even if you don't eat or drink here, it's a wonderful, bustling area to walk around. Piazza Navona is a natural meeting place, as is **Piazza della Rotonda** in front of the **Pantheon**. Finish the evening with an ice cream from **Tre Scalini** (▷ 151) or **Gelateria della Palma** (▷ 147).

SIGHTS AND EXPERIENCES

Palazzo Altemps (▷ 34)

This exquisite Renaissance palace plays host to some of the greatest of all Roman sculptures, among them Aphrodite's throne.

Palazzo-Galleria Doria Pamphilj (▷ 38)

This vast palace has more than 1,000 rooms and is home to a priceless collection of Italian art.

Pantheon (▷ 42)

Emperor Hadrian's temple is the world's best-preserved Roman monument, with an awe-inspiring entrance and a beautiful interior.

Piazza Campo de' Fiori (▷ 44)

The "Field of Flowers" is ringed with cafés and bars and holds a lively and colorful traditional food and flower market.

Piazza Navona (▷ 46)

Rome's most elegant piazza contains a church and fountains designed by baroque architects Bernini and Borromini.

Santa Maria sopra Minerva (▷ 54)

Discover a statue by Michelangelo and a sublime Renaissance fresco cycle in this lovely Gothic church.

MORE TO SEE	64

Colonna di Marco Aurelio
Crypta Balbi
Fontana delle Tartarughe
Museo Nazionale del Palazzo
  di Venezia

Palazzo Spada
San Luigi dei Francesi

CITY TOURS

Trastevere and the South

The former Ghetto and picturesque Trastevere area are more traditional quarters, full of narrow streets, local markets and neighborhood bars and restaurants.

Morning

Start at **Santa Maria in Cosmedin** (▷ 74), where you could try putting your hand in the Bocca della Verità in the porch—legend says that liars will get a hearty bite. Cross the road to admire the **Tempio di Vesta** and the **Tempio della Fortuna Virilis** (▷ 74–75) and then cut down to walk along the Lungotevere dei Pierleoni beside the river, with the Isola Tiberina ahead in the water. This will bring you to the end of Via Portico d'Ottavia, named for the ruins of a Roman gateway that stands here. It was built as part of a massive complex by Emperor Augustus in the first century BC and dedicated to his sister, Octavia. Today it forms part of the church of **Sant'Angelo in Pescheria**, to its left, which takes its name from the fish market that flourished on the site from Roman times until the Middle Ages.

Mid-morning

Explore the pretty labyrinth of little streets north of the Portico, then return to Via Portico d'Ottavia and follow it left and south past the Teatro di Marcello to the river and the synagogue and its **museum** (▷ 69). Cross the Ponte Fabricio (above) in front of you and walk around the **Isola Tiberina** (▷ 69), with a visit (if open) to the church of **San Bartolomeo**. Cross the Ponte Cestio to the Trastevere area. Not far from the bridge is **Santa Cecilia in Trastevere** (▷ 73).

Lunch

The most attractive part of Trastevere, and the area with the best choice of places for lunch, lies on the west side of Viale di Trastevere. You may want to eat here this evening, so consider a café snack or buy a picnic, perhaps from the stalls of the market in Piazza di San Cosimato.

Afternoon

After lunch, either explore some of the surrounding streets or head to the Lungotevere della Farnesina to take in the stunning waterside **Triumphs and Laments** (▷ 75) and the charming **Villa Farnesina** (▷ 62–63). If time allows, visit nearby **Palazzo Corsini** (right; ▷ 71) and/or take a break in the **Orto Botanico** (▷ 61), before heading down Via della Scala to take in the ancient church of **Santa Maria in Trastevere** (▷ 58–59).

Evening

Trastevere comes alive in the evenings, especially on and around Piazza di Santa Maria in Trastevere (left). Admire the floodlit mosaics on the facade of Santa Maria di Trastevere; enjoy the street life in the small lanes nearby; and perhaps take a drink in the earthy **Bar San Calisto** (▷ 133).

Dinner

Trastevere has many traditional-style restaurants, such as the quintessential **Da Augusto** (▷ 145), as well as a plethora of pizzerie, of which **Ivo** (▷ 148) and **Dar Poeta** (▷ 146) are classic examples. But it also has a new breed of contemporary dining options, such as **Glass Hostaria** (▷ 147), many of which are gathered around Piazza Trilussa.

CITY TOURS

Piazza Navona

ORSO DEL RINASCIMENTO

5

Palazzo Salviati

S Onofrio

Chiesa Nuova

via del Governo Vecchio

la Banchi Vecchi

via Giulia

CORSO VITTORIO EMANUELE II

via del Governo Vecchio

via del Pellegrino

S M di Monserato

Palazzo della Cancelleria

Sant'Andrea della Valle

Piazza di San Pantaleo

LUNGOTEVERE GIANICOLENSE

LUNGOTEVERE SANGALLO

via della Lungara

via degli Orti d'Albert

Via delle Mantellate

Largo Lorenzo Perosi

Ponte G Mazzini

S Eligio

via Giulia

S M di Cappellari

Piazza Campo de' Fiori

via Giubbonari

6

Francesco di Sales

Via di San Francesco di Sales

Via della Lungara

LUNGOTEVERE DEI TEBALDI

Tevere

Palazzo Falconieri

Palazzo Farnese

Piazza Farnese

Piazza della Querela

Palazzo Spada

Pettinari

Via dei Riari

Palazzo Corsini

Villa Farnesina

Triumphs and Laments

LUNGOTEVERE DELLA FARNESINA

Ponte Sisto

LUNGOTEVERE DEI VALLATI

Ministero della Giustizia

Roccoette

Monte Gianicolo

Orto Botanico

Palazzo Torlonia

VIA GARIBALDI

Via della Scala

Dar Poeta

Santa Maria della Scala

Glass Hostaria

Vicolo del Cinque

Via del Moro

Da Augusto

Piazza de' Renzi

Renella

LUNGOT DEI SANZIO

Piazza G G Belli

PONTE GARIBALDI

7

Porta S Pancrazio

Piazzale Aurelio

Via di Porta San Pancrazio

San Pietro in Montorio

VIA GARIBALDI

Vicolo del Cedro

S Egidio

Santa Maria in Trastevere

Piazza di S Maria in Trastevere

Bar San Calisto

S Crisogono

Bell della

Piazza Sidney Sonnino

Luce

Via A Masina

Via Giacomo Medici

Via P Roselli

Via Trenta Aprile

Via Goffredo Mameli

Ivo a Trastevere

Via Luciano Manara

Via di San Francesco a Ripa

Trastevere (Mastai)

VIA DI TRASTEVERE

Piazza Mastai

8

VIA LE DELLE MURA G IANICOLENSI

Via Nicola Fabrizi

Via G Sacchi

Piazza San Cosimato

Via N d Grande

★ **TRASTEVERE**

Via Calandrelli

VIALE GLORIOSO

Via E Morosini

Induno

VIA G INDUNO

San Francesco a Ripa

Porta Portese

Villa Sciarra

Via F Casini

Via Dandolo

Viale Aurelio Saffi

Trastevere (Min P Istruzione)

Viale delle Mura Portuensi

Piazza Porta Portese

G IANICOLENSI

VIA ALESSANDRO POERIO

Viale Aurelio Saffi

Trastevere (Bernardino da Feltre)

Via B Musolino

Via L'Orti di Trastevere

PORTUENSE

Portuense

TESTACCIO

Via G Rossetti

Via M Quadrio

9

Via G B Niccolini

Felice Cavallotti

Via Francesco

Via F Bandiera

Via U Bassi

Ippolito Nievo

Via N Parboni

LUNGOTEVERE

Via Rubattino

Via Florio

Via America

Via Fr D Guerrazzi

0 — 500 m

0 — 500 yds

D   E   F

Pantheon

Santa Maria
sopra Minerva

Palazzo-Galleria
Doria Pamphilj

Palazzo
Odescalchi

Santi
Apostoli

Palazzo
Colonna

Villa
Colonna

Le Domus
Romane

Largo
Magnanapoli

San Marco

Museo
Nazionale del
Palazzo di Venezia

Colonna
Traiana

Museo dei Fori
Imperiali e
Mercati di Traiano

Palazzo
Altieri

CORSO VITTORIO EMANUELE II

Templi
Repubblicani

Chiesa
del Gesù

Monumento
a Vittorio
Emanuele II

Piazza
Venezia

Fori
Imperiali

Santa Maria
in Aracoeli

Crypta
Balbi

Fontana delle
Tartarughe

Piazza del
Campidoglio

GHETTO

Musei
Capitolini

Arco di
Settimio
Severo

Santi Cosma
e Damiano

LUNGOTEVERE DEI CENCI

Teatro di
Marcello

Monte Capitolino

Foro
Romano

Arco di
Tito

Isola
Tiberina

Santa Nicola
in Carcere

S Teodoro

Orti
Farnesiani

San Bartolomeo
all' Isola

LUNGOT DELL' ANGUILLARA

PONTE
PALATINO

Tempio della
Fortuna Virilis

Monte Palatino

Casa di Livia

Tempio
di Vesta

Palazzo
dei Flavi

Sant'Anastasia

Domus
Augusti

Santa Maria
in Cosmedin

Santa Cecilia
in Trastevere

S Vincenzo
de Paoli

Circo
Massimo

AVENTINO

Circo Maximo
Experience

Tevere

S Alessio

S Prisca

Parco
di Porta
Capena

Emporio

Monte Aventino

S Anselmo

Marmorata
(Vanvitelli)

Aventino
(Albania)

Parco della
Resistenza
dell'8 Settembre

S Saba

97

CITY TOURS

Trastevere and the South
Quick Reference Guide

Santa Maria in Trastevere (▷ 58)

In a neighborhood of narrow streets, the 12th- to 13th-century church, with a Romanesque bell tower and mosaic-filled facade, and its square (Piazza Santa Maria in Trastevere) stand out. Both are especially lovely at night, when they are floodlit. The interior of the church is lined with Roman columns and baroque chapels under a sumptuous painted ceiling and a series of glittering mosaics.

Trastevere (▷ 60)

Trastevere means "across the Tiber" and you can cross a genuine Roman bridge, the Ponte Cestio, to reach this beguiling area. Once a blue-collar enclave, today it is a maze of picturesque streets, houses, bars, restaurants and quirky one-off stores, while its must-see sights include ancient churches such as Santa Maria in Trastevere, the Renaissance Villa Farnesina and the botanic garden.

Villa Farnesina (▷ 62)

Trastevere, for the most part, has historically been a poorer area of the city. Most of Rome's great palaces were built elsewhere. The Villa Farnesina is an exception, originally created for a Tuscan banker and later bought by the powerful Farnese family. More intimate than its neighbors across the river, it is best known for its lovely interior decoration, and for the frescoes designed and painted by Raphael and Baldassare Peruzzi.

CITY TOURS

Northern Rome

Northern Rome embraces historic and more recent areas of the city, as well as landmark sights such as Piazza di Spagna and the Fontana di Trevi. The area is also home to central Rome's principal park and several of its major galleries.

Morning

Most of northern Rome's sights are too far away and too widely separated to see in a single, coherent itinerary. Four are major galleries, two of which are probably enough for one day. If the Etruscans appeal, take a taxi to and from the **Villa Giulia** (▷ 70–71) and make this a self-contained visit. The same goes for the **Museo e Galleria Borghese** (right; ▷ 30–31), though here you could walk back toward the city through the **Villa Borghese** (▷ 75) and via the **Pincio** gardens (▷ 72) to Piazza del Popolo (to see **Santa Maria del Popolo**, ▷ 56–57) and from there along to **Piazza di Spagna** (▷ 48–49) on Via Margutta or Via del Babuino.

Mid-morning

Alternatively, you could walk from the Museo e Galleria Borghese directly to **Piazza di Spagna** (▷ 48–49), descending the Spanish Steps, where you'll find the **Museo Keats-Shelley** (▷ 70). This is another museum, but a small one, and its displays—devoted to the English Romantic poets and their circle—are in marked contrast to other galleries and museums of Roman, medieval or Renaissance art and sculpture in the area. If the museum does not appeal, take a break in one of the cafés on or near Piazza di Spagna or explore the many chic shops in the grid of streets around Via Condotti.

Lunch

Restaurants around Piazza di Spagna and Via Condotti tend to be on the expensive side. You'll find better value and much more choice west of **Via del Corso**, a slightly less exclusive shopping street. Better still, walk up Via Margutta, where you could eat fresh vegetarian food at **Margutta RistorArte** (▷ 148). Alternatively, there are plenty of other choices along Via del Babuino and cafés for a snack lunch in **Piazza del Popolo**.

Afternoon

If you have lunched near Piazza del Popolo, then you'll be well placed to see the controversial **Museo dell'Ara Pacis** (▷ 70). This will leave you slightly out on a limb, however, and you might prefer to make straight for the **Fontana di Trevi** (▷ 20–21), but be prepared for the crowds that throng the area around the fountain day and night. You are now reasonably close to the spooky **Santa Maria della Concezione** (▷ 74) and the grandiose **Palazzo Barberini** (▷ 36–37), which has art from a similar period to that in the Museo e Galleria Borghese.

Mid-afternoon

For something different, consider the Roman collection of the **Palazzo Massimo alle Terme** (above; ▷ 40–41), but take a bus or a taxi from Via del Tritone, as the walk—unless you wend through the backstreets between Via del Quirinale and Via Nazionale—is unappealing. The museum is close to Termini station.

Evening

At the end of a summer's day, there are few nicer places for a pre-dinner drink than the **Stravinskij Bar** (▷ 137), with its lovely courtyard garden. A few minutes' walk would then take you to **Matricianella** (▷ 148) for dinner, a restaurant that is well placed for an after-dinner stroll to admire the floodlit Trevi Fountain or to buy an ice cream at **Il Gelato di San Crispino** (right; ▷ 147), not far from the famous fountain.

VIALE BRUNO BUOZZI

Via C de Notaris

Via C Linneo

Via Michele Mercati

Via Antonio Gramsci

Via A Mangilli

Belle Arti Sant'Eugenio

Museo Etrusco / Villa Giulia

Via di Villa Giulia

VIALE DELLE

ULISSE ALDROVANDI

Aldrovandi

Via di Villa Giulia

Belle Arti

Via Flaminia

Museo Nazionale Etrusco di Villa Giulia

Acc di Roma

Galleria Nazionale d'Arte Moderna e Contemporanea

Bioparco di Roma

BELLE

Valle Giulia

ARTI

Viale del Giardino

Ist Storico Olandese

Acc Belgica

Galleria Arte Moderna

Piazzale Firdusi

Viale del Giulia

Museo Pietro Canonica

Via P S G Marri

Piazza della Marina

Ministero Marina

Via M Fortuny

Via M Camozzi

Azuni (Min Marina)

Via D A Azuni

Via Flaminia

Villa Strohl Fern

Viale Esculapio

Via Pietro Canonica

Piazza di Siena

Via P S G Marti

Via degli Scialoja

STAZIONE ROMA FLAMINIO

Viale Washington

Viale Fiorello La Guardia

Via Cesare Beccaria

Via F Carrara

Flaminio Piazza del Popolo

Piazzale Flaminio

VIALE

Piazzale delle Canestre

Viale San Paolo del Braolo

Via L DI SAVOIA

Piazza del Popolo

★ **Santa Maria del Popolo** *Pincio*

DEL

Viale delle Magnolie

Galoppatoio

Via Maria Adelaide

Stravinskij Bar

Viale Trinità

MURO

Villa Medici

Viale del

TORTO

Calcopatoio

PONTE REGINA MARGHERITA

LUNGOTEVERE IN AUGUSTA

Via A Brunetti

Passeggiata di Ripetta

Via del Vantaggio

Museo di Goethe

Via Margutta

Margutta RistorArte

Tevere

Via M Clementi

Via Ripetta

Via della Frezza

Via dei Greci

Via Vittoria

Via del Babuino

SS Trinità dei Monti

Via Porta Pinciana

Via M M Dionigi

VIA V COLONNA

PONTE CAVOUR

Piazza Augusto Imperatore

Mausoleo di Augusto

Via della Croce

Via della Carrozze

Piazza di Spagna

Spagna

Museo Keats-Shelley

S Isidoro

Museo dell'Ara Pacis

SS Ambrogio e Carlo al Corso

Via dell'Arancio

Via Tomacelli

Via delle Bocca di Leone

Via dei Condotti

Via Borgognona

Via F Crispi

Via Gregoriana

Via C le Case

Via Due Macelli

Via Sistina

Palazzo Borghese

Via Fontanella Borghese

Palazzo Ruspoli Matricianella

Via Frattina

Via della Vite

Via delle Fontanella

San Lorenzo in Lucina

Via della Mercede

TRITONE

Via Monte Brianzo

LUNGOTEVERE MARZIO

Via dei Prefetti

Via della Scrofa

Piazza Parlamento

Piazza di S Silvestro

Accademia di San Luca

Il Gelato di San Crispino

Via dell'Orso

La Maddalena

Via di Campo Marzio

Piazza di Montecitorio

Palazzo di Montecitorio

Palazzo Chigi

Palazzo della Stamperia

Fontana di Trevi

Palazzo Altemps

Via Zanardelli

Piazza Cinque Lune

San Luigi dei Francesi

CORSO DEL RINASCIMENTO

Sant'Eustachio in Campo Marzio

Colonna di Marco Aurelio

Piazza Colonna

Piazza Montecitorio

Via delle Muratte

Palazzo del Quirinale

Via della Dataria

Piazza del Quirinale

Palazzo Consulta

Piazza Navona

Piazza della Rotonda

Via dei Pastini

Sant'Ignazio di Loyola

Palazzo Sciarra

Via dell'Umiltà

Santi Apostoli

Villa Colonna

Monterone

Pantheon

Piazza Sant'Eustachio

Santa Maria sopra Minerva

Palazzo Odescalchi

Palazzo Colonna

Piazza Minerva

Palazzo-Galleria Doria Pamphilj

F   G   H

Northern Rome Quick Reference Guide

SIGHTS AND EXPERIENCES

Fontana di Trevi (▷ 20)
Throw a coin into Rome's prettiest and most famous fountain and legend says that you will be sure to return to the city.

Museo e Galleria Borghese (▷ 30)
You need to pre-book your visit to enjoy the beauty of the Borghese palace, its paintings and sculptures.

Palazzo Barberini (▷ 36)
Paintings by Caravaggio and Raphael form part of the collection of art and antiquities in this lavishly decorated baroque palace.

Palazzo Massimo alle Terme (▷ 40)
See some of the city's best Roman and Greek frescoes, murals and sculpture in an elegant 19th-century palazzo.

Piazza di Spagna (▷ 48)
The Piazza di Spagna is the setting for one of Rome's great sights, the Spanish Steps, and the focus of the city's luxury shopping district.

Santa Maria del Popolo (▷ 56)
One of Rome's most atmospheric small churches has sculptures by Jacopo Sansovino and paintings by Pinturicchio and Caravaggio.

CITY TOURS

Vatican and Around

Vatican City is an independent state that is home to St. Peter's and the Vatican Museums, a vast complex that contains the Sistine Chapel. Close by is the Castel Sant'Angelo, whose long history has seen it used as a mausoleum, fortress, prison and museum.

Morning
Lines for the **Musei Vaticani** (right; ▷ 26–27) can be extremely long, whatever the time of year, so arrive as early as possible, or book ahead online. You will probably need most of the morning simply to see the highlights of the various museums, but note that you will not be allowed to spend long in the **Cappella Sistina**—such is the weight of people wanting to see Michelangelo's famous frescoes that visitors are constantly kept on the move.

Mid-morning
The museums have a café if you wish to take a break from the more than 11km (7 miles) of galleries that make up the complex.

Lunch
Exit the museums and turn right down the hill to Piazza del Risorgimento, which has a selection of mediocre cafés and pizzerias. Better options are to the north (try **Dal Toscano** ▷ 146, in Via Germanico) or head towards the Ottaviano metro station; there are some good choices along here, including **Pizzarium Bonci** (▷ 149), though this is take-out only. Restaurants in this area are likely to be busy.

Afternoon

It is an easy walk from the Musei Vaticani to Piazza San Pietro (left) and the **Basilica di San Pietro** (▷ 14–15). You will have to stand in line on the northwest side of the piazza for a security screening before entering the basilica. Lines are shorter later in the afternoon, but note that the church usually closes at 7pm or earlier. This said, you probably won't need to spend more than an hour in the church unless you wish to climb the dome.

This leaves time to visit the **Castel Sant'Angelo** (▷ 16–17), a walk along Via della Conciliazione. If you didn't want to see the Vatican Museums, an easy alternative itinerary might see you visiting the Castel early in the morning and the basilica before lunch.

Evening

You should make an effort to linger in—or return to—**Piazza San Pietro** in the evening to enjoy the piazza and the basilica (right) under floodlights. The area does not have as many good dining possibilities as the rest of central Rome, but you can enjoy a light and elegant meal with a superb choice of wines at **Del Frate** (▷ 146). Or head for **La Pratolina** (▷ 150), a great choice for sampling some very special pizza called *pinsa*, and generally buzzing with Romans and visitors.

TRIONFALE

Via Premuda
Via Emilio Faà di Bruno
Via Cunfida
Via C Morin
Via G Bettolo
VIA DELLA GIULIANA

S Giusep

CIRCONVALLAZIONE TRIONFALE
Via San Tommaso d'Aquino
Via G Bovio
Via B C Telesio
Via Rodi
Via San Buccari
Trionfale
Campanella
Savonarola
Giordano Bruno

VIALE DELLE MEDAGLIE D'ORO
Via A Labriola
Via U Bartolomei
Via Simone Simoni
Via C Passaglia

VIA ANDREA DORIA
Via Famagosta
Via Ottranto
VIA LEONE IV
Via Tolemaide
Santamaura
Via la Goletta
Via Mocenigo
Via Ruggero di Lauria
Via V Pisani

Piazzale degli Eroi

Musei

VIA CIPRO
Via C Venticinque

Via Luigi Rizzo
Via Pietro Ziani
Via Sebastiano

Via F Albenzio
CANDIA
Via Sebastiano Veniero
Via Tunisi

Piazza di S Maria delle Grazie

Cipro
Pizzarium Bonci

Dal Toscano

VIALE B DI MICHELANGELO

Santa Maria delle Grazie

Via Vaticano

Museo Gregoriano Etrusco

★ Musei Vaticani

Giardini Vaticani

VIA ANGELO EMO
Via Mercantonio Bragadin
Via Giorgio Scalia
Viale degli Ammiragli
Via D Millelire

S M Mediatrice

Via Vaticano

Casina di Pio IV

CITTÀ DEL VATICANO

★ Cappella Sistina

Palazzo del Governatorato

★ Basilica di San Pietro

Piazza San Pietro

STAZIONE VATICANO

Viale Vaticano
Via Nicolò V

Palazzo del Sant'Uffizio

Aula delle Udienze

Porta Cavallegger

VIA AURELIA
Via di Villa Alberici
Via di Paolo III

AURELIA

VIA DI PORTA CAVALLEGGERI

VIA DEL CROCIFISSO
Via Paolo II
Via Nicolò II di
Stazione
VIA DELLE FORNACI
Via S de Gasperi
Via A de Gasperi

S Maria alle Fornaci

S Maria Mediatrice

Campi Sportivi

Clivo di Monte del Gallo
Via del Cottolengo
VIA GREGORIO VII
VIA INNOCENZO III
Via Pietro
Via P Doria
VIA STAZIONE DI SAN PIETRO

STAZIONE ROMA SAN PIETRO

| 0 | | 500 m |
| 0 | | 500 yds |

VIA GREGORIO VII
Via Evaristo
San D'Amaso

Monte del Gallo

Maria Addolorata

Via A Ceriani
Via S Silverio

The Vatican and Around
Quick Reference Guide

CITY TOURS

Basilica di San Pietro (▷ 14)

St. Peter's Basilica was built over the site where the Apostle St. Peter was supposedly buried in the first century. The current church, created over a century, replaced an older church founded around AD326. Piazza San Pietro provides a grand setting for the church, whose vast interior contains a wealth of art and decoration, including Michelangelo's sculptural masterpiece, the *Pietà*.

Castel Sant'Angelo (▷ 16)

The circular bastion of the Castel Sant'Angelo has dominated the banks of the River Tiber since AD130, when the Emperor Hadrian built it as a mausoleum for himself and his imperial successors. In time it became a papal fortress, connected to the Vatican by a covered passageway, and later a prison and a barracks. Today, it is a museum, offering a wide range of papal, military and other exhibits.

Musei Vaticani e Cappella Sistina (▷ 26)

The world's largest museum complex contains many of the artistic treasures accumulated by the papacy in the course of almost 2,000 years. The Sistine Chapel, which lies within the complex, is covered in frescoes by some of the greatest painters of their day, and overarched by Michelangelo's ceiling fresco and his painting of the *Last Judgment*.

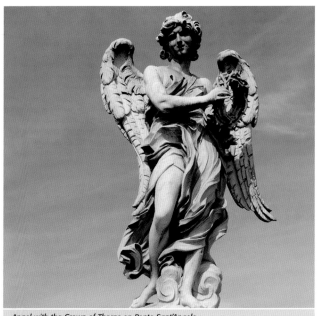

Angel with the Crown of Thorns on Ponte Sant'Angelo

CITY TOURS

Farther Afield

Rome's periphery contains several historical sights, notably a fine bath complex and a cluster of catacombs on the Via Appia Antica. To the east, Tivoli, home to three villas, is one of Rome's most popular excursions. Both of these itineraries can be done as day trips.

DAY 1 Morning

A long morning can quite easily be devoted to the sights that are gathered conveniently south and southeast of the city center. Start by taking a bus (75 or 118) or the metro to see the **Circo Massimo** (▷ 66), a large open area that was once a Roman racetrack, and then the **Terme di Caracalla** (right; ▷ 77), an ancient bath complex.

Mid-morning

Take bus 118, 160 or 628 from the Terme to the cluster of sights concentrated on or near the Via Appia Antica, the well-preserved remains of one of ancient Rome's earliest roads. Here you can see the **catacombs of San Callisto and San Sebastiano** (▷ 76), along with the roadside tombs of eminent ancient Romans such as Geta and Cecilia Metella. Not far away are three more catacombs, the **Catacombe Ebraiche** (Jewish Catacombs), **Catacombe di San Domitilla** and **Catacombe di Prestato**.

Lunch

It makes sense to pack a lunch to eat on the **Via Appia Antica** (left). Alternatively, the area near the start of the Via Appia Antica, around the church of the **Domine Quo Vadis**, has cafés and one or two restaurants, notably **Priscilla** (▷ 150).

Afternoon

Return by bus 118 to Piazza della Bocca della Verità. Cross the river to Lungotevere dell'Anguillara, where you can pick up bus 125 to the corner of Via Garibaldi and Via di Porta di San Pancrazio for a short uphill walk to **Monte Gianicolo** (▷ 76–77). On your return, either take the same bus 125 or walk back through Trastevere.

DAY 2 Morning

A visit to **Tivoli** (▷ 79) makes the most of a full day, but avoid Mondays, when some sights are shut, and, if possible, weekends, when the town is especially busy with Roman day-trippers. A train from Termini is the best way to get there—take the earliest you can manage and remember to validate your train tickets by punching them in the platform machines. On arrival, make straight for the town's well-signed main villa and garden, the **Villa d'Este** (▷ 79).

Mid-morning

The **Villa d'Este** (left) could easily occupy you all morning, but if you still have an hour or so before lunch, consider seeing the town's second villa, the **Villa Gregoriana** (▷ 79), on the opposite (eastern) side of Tivoli.

Lunch

Tivoli sees many visitors, and offers numerous, often poor-quality cafés and restaurants. **Ristorante Sibilla** (▷ 150), which dates from 1730, used to be one of these, but the quality of the food and service has recently improved, and the views from the terrace garden over the Aniene gorge are as good as ever. It's also convenient for the Villa Gregoriana if you didn't see it in the morning.

Afternoon

After lunch, return to Piazza Garibaldi, Tivoli's main square, where you can pick up a bus (CAT 4 or 4X) to the third of Tivoli's main attractions, the spacious **Villa Adriana** (right; ▷ 79), whose extensive site should easily keep you occupied for the whole afternoon. Return to Tivoli by bus 4 or 4X and then take the train back to Termini (or use bus and metro).

Osteria
Nuova

Olgiata

C Mal
Borghetto

Tragliatella

Ísola
Farnese

Parco
Regionale
di Veio

La Storta

2

2 bis

Prima
Porta

La Giustiniana

Tragliata

Tomba di
Nerone

Ottavia

A90

S ONÓFRIO

TORREVÉCCHIA

Arrone

PRIMAVALLE

MAXXI

Casalotti

Castel di
Guido

Montespaccato

CITTÀ DEL
VATICANO

*Monte
Gianicolo*

Massimina

**Villa Doria
Pamphilj**

CORVIALE

Malagrotta

Casetta
Mattei

**San Paolo
Fuori le Mura**

A12

E80

TRULLO
MAGLIANA

*Riserva
Naturale Statale
Litorale Romano*

Ponte
Galeria

A91

**Aeroporto
Intercontinentale
Leonardo da Vinci-
Fiumicino**

Tevere

A90

Acilia Nord

Tor de' Cenci

Vitinia

Vallerano

Fiumicino

Ostia
Antica

8

Casal
Palocco

VIA CRISTOFORO COLOMBO

**Ostia
Antica**

Lido di
Ostia Levante

Castel
Porziano

148

Trigória
Alta

*Riserva
Naturale
di Decima
Malafede*

*Riserva
Naturale
Statale Tenuta
di Castel Porziano*

Castel
Romano

Cascina
Capocotta

| 0 | | 5 km |
| 0 | | 3 miles |

Settebagni

Riserva Naturale della Marcigliana

Marcigliana

Riserva Naturale Nomentum

Montecelio

A1 dir

Guidonia

TUFELLO
Aeroporto di Roma-Urbe

A90

Tor Lupara

A1

Bagni di Tivoli

MONTE SACRO

SAN BASILIO

Settecamini

Villalba

S MARIA D SOCCORSE

Tor Cervara

Lunghezza

Aniene

A24

E45

ROMA

TOR SAPIENZA

Terme di Caracalla

CENTOCELLE

Colle del Sole

Valle Martella

GARBATELLA

Torre Angela

6

Finocchio

Catacombe di San Callisto

CINECITTÀ

Torre Gaia

Catacome di San Sebastiano

Parco Regionale dell' Appia Antica

7

A1 dir

Colonna

Cecchignola

Morena

Frascati

Monte Compatri

Aeroporto Intercontinentale di Ciampino

Ciampino

Grottaferrata

Castel di Leva

Santa Maria delle Mole

Marino

Rocca di Papa

Falcognana

Frattocchie

Parco Regionale dei Castelli Romani

Lago Albano

Castel Gandolfo

Pavona

Albano Laziale

Nemi

Aríccia

Lago di Nemi

Santa Palomba

207

Genzano di Roma

Cecchina

7

Pomezia

SIGHTS AND EXPERIENCES

Ostia Antica (▷ 32–33)
The present Ostia lies not far from Fiumicino airport, southwest of central Rome. Today, it is a small town and modest seaside resort, but 2,000 years ago its ancient Roman counterpart, Ostia Antica—now some way inland—was the main port for the imperial city. The conduit for the immense trade and riches of empire, it rose to prominence in the fourth century BC, and remained Rome's port for around 600 years. As the coast receded it became landlocked and was eventually all but covered in silt and mud. Archaeological excavations have since revealed remarkable remains.

MORE TO SEE	64

Catacombe di San Callisto
Catacombe di San Sebastiano
MAXXI
Monte Gianicolo
San Paolo Fuori le Mura
Terme di Caracalla
Villa Doria Pamphilj

ENTERTAINMENT	128

Bars and Clubs
Co.So.
Lanficio 159

Sports
Stadio Olimpico

EAT	138

Bars by Day
Bar Necci dal 1924
Roman/Italian
Cacciani

Priscilla
Ristorante Sibilla
Zarazà

Shop

Whether you're looking for the best local products, a department store or a quirky boutique, you'll find them all in Rome. In this section, shops are listed alphabetically.

SHOP

Introduction

Rome was once the marketplace of an empire that embraced much of the known world. Today, its shops are tempting enough to provide a serious distraction from the city's cultural delights. All the great Italian retail staples—food, wine, fashion, shoes, leatherware and clothing—are well represented, and the city is a good source of art, antiques and artisan products.

More for your Money

Mid-price shoes and clothes represent good value for money; you will find them in countless shops around the new city, but particularly Via Nazionale, Via del Tritone and Via del Corso. The same streets are also dotted with small specialist shops selling good-quality bags, gloves and other leatherware. The market near Piazza Vittorio Emanuele II, where many Romans shop, is good for clothes and shoes, as well as pots, pans and kitchenware with an Italian stamp. In stylish Rome, even inexpensive clothes tend to be good quality and well cut.

Designer Names

At the other sartorial extreme, most of the great Italian and other European fashion houses have shops in the city: Gucci, Prada and Armani are all here, in the grid of streets around Via dei

---

ANTIQUES

It is no wonder, given Rome's long history, that the city is a treasury of antiques. Prices are often high, but the range of objects—Etruscan, Roman, Renaissance, baroque and other items—is unrivaled. For paintings and prints, head for Via Margutta, which also has galleries selling contemporary art and carpets. For general antiques, try Via Giulia, Via del Babuino (Persian carpets), Via dei Coronari, Via dell'Orso and Via del Monserrato. Also good, and with lower prices and less exclusive stock, are Via del Panico, Via del Pellegrino and Via dei Banchi Nuovi. Note you will need a licence to export any antiques out of the country.

Clockwise from top: Window shopping near Piazza San Lorenzo; an attractive arrangement of bottled liqueurs; hats on a stall in Trastevere; shop in style on

Condotti, an excellent source of high-class clothes, shoes, lingerie and accessories. Department stores have never caught on, and only Coin and Rinascente are worth a visit.

Tempt your Taste Buds

Shopping for food has a unique charm in Rome, whether in the small local shops known as *alimentari*, or the specialist delicatessens in streets such as Via della Croce. The markets, particularly Campo de' Fiori, are vibrant sources of provisions. Pasta, the finest extra virgin oil, *funghi porcini* (dried cep mushrooms), truffle oil and spices make good food buys.

Religious Items

The range of shops selling religious items is vast. The largest concentration is around St. Peter's—look out for ceramic Swiss Guards and fluorescent rosaries. On Via dei Cestari all manner of ecclesiastic garb is available—if you ever daydreamed about buying a bishop's robe or a cardinal's hat, this is the place.

Fun for the Visitor

Rome has any number of shops and stalls selling plaster and plastic casts of famous statues. Stores around the tourist traps sell inexpensive souvenirs, from figures of gladiators to models of the Colosseum. Better-quality items, plus books, prints and artistic replicas, are sold in museum and gallery shops.

MARBLED PAPER

Notebooks and other stationery items covered with marbled paper make wonderful souvenirs, and can be found all over the city. The paper originated in Venice, where the technique arrived from the East in the 15th century, and is still often handmade. The process involves floating multicolor pigments on liquid gum and combing the different colors into distinctive patterns. The paper is placed delicately on top, then lifted and hung up to dry.

Via dei Condotti, a great place for designer clothes and accessories; cooked meats at a deli on Via Marmorata; religious statues for sale near St. Peter's Basilica

Directory

THE ANCIENT CITY
Department Stores
Coin
Food and Wine
Bottega del Cioccolato
Panella

CENTRAL ROME
Accessories and Leather Goods
Ibiz – Artigianato in Cuio
Beauty
L'Olfattorio
Books and Stationery
Aldo Fefè
Cartoleria Pantheon
Poggi
Fashion
Le Artigiane
Fabindia
SBU
Footwear
Borini
Interiors
Bartolucci
Bassetti
De Sanctis

TRASTEVERE AND THE SOUTH
Books and Stationery
Almost Corner Bookshop
Fashion
La Cravatta su Misura
Food and Wine
Drogheria Innocenzi

NORTHERN ROME
Accessories and Leather Goods
Gucci
Books and Stationery
Pineider
Department Stores
La Rinascente
Interiors
Bottega di Marmoraro
C.U.C.I.N.A.
Men's Fashion
Ermenegildo Zegna
Women's Fashion
Marella

VATICAN AND AROUND
Food and Wine
Castroni
Franchi

Shopping A–Z

ALDO FEFÈ

The family owners have been in the business of creating lovely stationery items using their hand-painted papers since the 1930s, and you'll find everything from single sheets of paper, good enough to frame, through desk paraphernalia to picture frames and photo albums. Much of the work is done in the shop, so you can watch the process while you browse.

➕ F5 ✉ Via della Stelletta 20B ☎ 06 6880 3585 ⏰ Mon–Sat 8–7.30

ALMOST CORNER BOOKSHOP

This tiny bookshop stocks an interesting and unusual selection of English-language books. The prices are competitive, and it is particularly good on biography and history, with a strong emphasis on Rome and Italy. Staff are both helpful and knowledgeable.

➕ E7 ✉ Via del Moro 45 ☎ 06 583 6942 ⏰ Mon–Sat 11–7, Sun 11–4. Closed Sun in Aug

LE ARTIGIANE

leartigiane.it

Italy is anxious to promote artisan producers of every type and this treasure-crammed store has a great range of eclectic offerings, the work of local artisans. Browse for everything from clothes and one-off pieces of jewelry to home accessories and lighting.

➕ F5 ✉ Via di Torre Argentina 72 ☎ 06 6830 9347 ⏰ Mon–Sat 10–7

BARTOLUCCI

bartolucci.com

Bartolucci are renowned wood carvers, with shops in different parts of Italy. Everything in store is hand carved, and it's hard to resist the cheery clocks, toys, various kitchen bits and pieces and Pinocchios—a house specialty that comes in all sizes. This is one of two outlets in Rome.

➕ G5 ✉ Piazza Navona 53; Viale delle Colli Portuense ☎ 06 6919 0894; 06 7657 44143 ⏰ Daily 10–10

BASSETTI

fratellibassetti.com

Italy has a long tradition of dress-making and bespoke tailoring, and many Romans have their clothes custom made. Bassetti is where they come to buy the fabrics, and there's a bewildering range of every conceivable textile at this enticing store. You'll find bolts of silk, wool, jersey, linen, cotton and brocade, as well as wonderful accessories and household linens of all descriptions.

➕ G6 ✉ Via delle Botteghe Oscure 51 ☎ 06 689 2325 ⏰ Tue–Fri 9.30–7.30, Sat 10–7, Mon 3.30–7.30

Window-shopping

BORINI

Shoes are piled everywhere in this gloriously crammed shop, with something on offer in myriad colors for every occasion and every taste. Expect value for money and shoes that will last.

F5 ✉ Via dei Pettinari 86 ☎ 06 687 5670 ⏰ Tue–Sat 10–7.30, Mon 11–7.30

BOTTEGA DEL CIOCCOLATO

labottegadelcioccolato.it

Most goodies in this chocolate shop are produced from a 19th-century Piedmontese recipe; others are "secrets of old masters." There are period cupboards and shelves, and a mirror reflects the chocolate creations in jars along the wall. There's a second outlet at Via del Vantaggio 22a.

J6 ✉ Via Leonina 82 ☎ 06 482 1473 ⏰ Mon–Sat 9.30–7.30. Closed mid-Jun to Sep

BOTTEGA DI MARMORARO

It's nice to know that marble, beloved of the Roman emperors, is still worked today in Rome. This tiny shop-cum-workshop is dedicated to restoring and sourcing antique marble, but also pulls in visitors searching for an original souvenir—a marble plaque or tablet engraved with any inscription you like in Latin or Italian.

G3 ✉ Via Margutta 53b ☎ 06 320 7660 ⏰ Mon–Sat 8–7.30

CARTOLERIA PANTHEON

pantheon-roma.com

Founded in 1910, this stationery shop sells hand-crafted writing materials of every type. Notebooks, albums and address books are bound in soft leather or marbled paper, and they also offer a vast variety of writing accessories and bags. If you've always wanted a quill pen or a customized seal for wax, this is the place to come.

F5 ✉ Via della Maddalena 41 ☎ 06 687 5633 ⏰ Mon–Fri 10.30–8, Sun 1–8

CASTRONI

castroni.com

Castroni boasts Rome's largest selection of imported delicacies, a mouthwatering array of Italian specialties, the finest wines and oils and a wide range of coffees. It has 12 outlets around the city.

D3 ✉ Via Cola di Rienzo 196–198, corner of Via Terenzio ☎ 06 687 4383 ⏰ Mon–Sat 8–8

COIN

coin.it

One of Rome's most popular department stores, Coin has a wide choice of cosmetics, home furnishings, kitchenware, toys and fashions. The top floor is dedicated to home exhibitions. There is another branch, complete with food hall, on Via Cola di Rienzo in Trastevere.

GIFTS WITH A TWIST

For a souvenir with a difference, visit the extraordinary shops on Via dei Cestari, just south of the Pantheon, which specialize in all sorts of religious clothes, candles and vestments. Crucifixes, rosaries, statues of saints and other religious souvenirs can be found in shops on Via di Porta Angelica near the Vatican. If unique, cutting-edge design or fabulous vintage clothing appeals, head for the delights of the independent boutiques of Via del Governo Vecchio, just off Piazza Navona.

M8 ✉ Piazzale Appio 7 ☎ 06 708 0020 ⏰ Mon–Sat 10–8.30, Sun 10.30–8.30

LA CRAVATTA SU MISURA

cravattasumisura.it

Italian style is to the fore at this store, with multi-hued ties in finest Italian silk and British wool. They can make you a beautiful piece of neckwear to your own specifications in a day or so—or, if pushed, in a few hours.

F8 ✉ Via di Santa Cecilia 12 ☎ 06 8901 6941 ⏰ Mon–Fri 10–7, Sat 10–2; also Dec Sun 10–2. Closed Aug

C.U.C.I.N.A.

cucinastore.com

A series of long, narrow rooms opens up as you enter this temple to kitchenwares and gadgetry. Pots, pans, molds, pasta-makers, dishes, bowls and platters are piled high and every spare corner is filled with incredibly tempting kitchen aids you didn't realize you needed, from truffle slicers to bamboo rice steamers.

G3 ✉ Via Mario de' Fiori 65 ☎ 06 679 1275 ⏰ Tue–Fri 10–7.30, Sat 10.30–7.30, Sun–Mon 11.30–7.30

DE SANCTIS

desanctis1890.com

Italy's wonderfully vibrant and colorful ceramics are hand crafted all over the country and this store sells pottery of every type from Tuscany, Umbria, Sicily and elsewhere. You can decorate your home and stock your kitchen and dining room, all at prices that may be surprisingly affordable. They also offer a shipping service for heavier items.

G5 ✉ Piazza di Pietra 24 ☎ 06 6880 6810 ⏰ Mon–Sat 10–1.30, 3–7.30

DROGHERIA INNOCENZI

Right on bustling Piazza San Cosimato in the heart of Trastevere, this foodie's haven is stacked to the ceiling with sacks of pasta and polenta, regional specialties such as honey and olive oil, and products from abroad that are difficult to find elsewhere, from Japanese miso soup to German mustard. People travel from far and wide to stock up here.

E8 ✉ Piazza San Cosimato, corner of Via Natale del Grande 31 ☎ 06 581 2725 ⏰ Daily 8.30–1.30, 4.30–8; closed Thu pm and part of Aug

ERMENEGILDO ZEGNA

zegna.com

This is generally considered to be one of Rome's top menswear stores. The accent here is on quintessential Italian style, where the casual clothes are as elegant as the tailored ones. Come here for informal suits and jackets in exquisite, expensive fabrics, as well as stylish shirts, cashmere sweaters and accessories.

G4 ✉ Via dei Condotti 58 ☎ 06 6994 0678 ⏰ Mon–Sat 10–7.30, Sun 10–7

SHOP

FABINDIA
fabindia.it

Facing the Ponte Sant'Angelo is this delightful emporium selling Indian fabrics, scarves and garments, all handwoven and made in Indian villages. The company is devoted to developing fair and equitable relationships with the producers. The styles are both traditional and more contemporary, and textiles range from the finest, lightest silks to heavy embroidered cottons.

✚ E5 ✉ Via del Banco di Santo Spirito 40 ☎ 06 6889 1230 ◷ Mon–Sat 10–1.30, 3–7.30, Sun 11–7

FRANCHI
franchi.it

This is one of the best delis in town, with everything on offer from salamis, antipasti, cheeses and wines to succulent roast meats, fish, salads and sumptuous delicacies for a picnic.

✚ D3 ✉ Via Cola di Rienzo 200/204 ☎ 06 686 5564 ◷ Daily 7.30–9

ROMAN MARKETS

Rome's daily food markets are good places to rustle together a picnic, grab some take-home food gifts or add a few iconic images to the holiday snapshot collection. For sheer picturesque charm, Campo de' Fiori heads the list, but don't miss San Cosimato in Trastevere or the Nuovo Mercato in happening Testaccio. Weekends see a fabulous farmers' market, known as the Mercato Campagna Amica, near the Circo Massimo, selling produce from the countryside around Rome, and Via Porta Pratese pulls in the crowds on Sundays for its famous flea market. For bags, shoes and inexpensive clothes head to the Mercato di Via Sannio, right by San Giovanni in Laterano.

GUCCI
gucci.com

This world-famous name originally specialized in equestrian leather work, and you can still see traces of this in the iconic buckles, straps and detailing on the high-end bags, shoes and accessories for both men and women.

✚ G3 ✉ Via Condotti 8 ☎ 06 679 0405 ◷ Mon–Sat 10–7.30, Sun 11–7

IBIZ – ARTIGIANATO IN CUIO
ibizroma.it

This family-run leather shop crafts butter-soft bags, belts, wallets and accessories in myriad jewel-bright colors. Designs are simple and practical, with elegant, capacious bags coming in at around €100–€140.

✚ F6 ✉ Via dei Chiavari 39 ☎ 06 6830 7297 ◷ Mon–Sat 9.30–7.30

MARELLA
marella.com

Understated, easy elegance is Marella's key look, and you'll find a wide range of their latest designs at this flagship store. Their designs are classic with a twist and offer excellent value for money. There is also an outlet on Via Solferino.

✚ G4 ✉ Via Frattina 129–31 ☎ 06 6992 3800 ◷ Tue–Sat 10–7.30, Mon, Sun 11–2, 3–7

L'OLFATTORIO
olfattorio.it

This delightful store stocks essences from names such as Diptyque, Artisan Parfumeur and Coudray, which the knowledgeable staff will blend, with your help, into a bespoke fragrance just for you—a memorable experience for which it's wise to book ahead.

Roman supermarkets are few and far between and most food is still bought in tiny local shops known as *alimentari*. Every street of every "village" or district in the city has one or more of these general shops, a source of everything from olive oil and pasta to corn and bunion treatments. They are also good places to buy picnic provisions—many sell bread and wine—and most have a delicatessen counter that will make you a sandwich *(panino)* from the meats and cheeses on display. For something a little more special, or for food gifts to take home, visit Via della Croce, a street renowned for its wonderful delicatessens.

🔲 G5 ✉ Via di Ripetta 34 ☎ 06 361 2325 🕐 Daily 10–7.30

PANELLA

panellaroma.com

For more than a century, Panella, located in the heart of Rome, has sold dozens of varieties of bread and cakes, and it has the largest selection of homemade *grissini* (bread sticks) in Rome. The back rooms are packed with hard-to-find ingredients. There's also a bar and café, with pleasant tables on the terrace outside (heated in winter).

🔲 K6 ✉ Via Merulana 54–55 ☎ 06 487 2435 🕐 Mon–Thu 8am–11pm, Fri–Sat 8am–midnight, Sun 8.30–4

PINEIDER

pineider.com

Pineider, Rome's most exclusive stationer, ships worldwide, so if you buy here you can reorder online. They sell beautiful high-quality leather office bags and cases, wallets, fine pencils and pens, but are most noted for their huge range of stationery—writing paper, notecards, notebooks and bookmarks are all on offer, sold either as boxed sets or individually. They will print personalized headings and have a wide choice of visiting card designs.

🔲 H4 ✉ Via dei Due Macelli 68 ☎ 06 678 9013 🕐 Mon–Sat 10–7

POGGI

poggi1825.it

Vivid pigments, lovely papers and canvases and exquisitely soft brushes have been on sale at Poggi's since 1825. A second shop in Trastevere sells a range of high-quality paper.

🔲 G5 ✉ Via del Gesù 74–75 ☎ 06 679 3674 🕐 Mon–Sat 9–2, 3–7.30

🔲 F8 ✉ Via Cardinal Merry del Val 18/19 ☎ 06 581 2531 🕐 Mon–Sat 10–7.30

LA RINASCENTE

rinascente.it

Italy's chicest one-stop fashion chain has its flagship store in the heart of Rome. There's another branch on Piazza del Fiume.

🔲 H4 ✉ Via del Tritone 61 ☎ 06 879 161 🕐 Daily 10–9

SBU

sbu.it

If you're tracking down cutting-edge Roman style, head to this converted 19th-century workshop, the headquarters of Strategic Business Unit, famed for its superbly cut jeans. These are mainly made in Italy from the finest Japanese denim, but there are Japanese pieces too, plus shirts, sweaters, jackets, women's wear and interesting jewelry.

🔲 F5 ✉ Via di San Pantaleo 68–69 ☎ 06 6880 2547 🕐 Mon–Sat 10–7.30

SHOP

Entertainment

Once you've done with sightseeing for the day, you'll find lots of other great things to do with your time in this chapter, even if all you want to do is relax with a drink. In this section, establishments are listed alphabetically.

Introduction

In such a striking city, and one whose climate is so benign, a stroll on a balmy evening might be all the entertainment you need. At the same time, Rome offers world-class classical concerts, recitals in churches, and plenty of jazz, blues and other live music. Films and productions in Italian mean cinema and theater are less accessible to most visitors, but opera and sport—notably football and rugby's Six Nations—transcend language. So, too, do the pleasures of a late-night drink or dance in one of the city's many bars and clubs.

Locations

City-center nightlife focuses on the streets around Piazza Navona (▷ 46–47), and the Campo de' Fiori, home to numerous bars, clubs and restaurants. They're buzzing, with an increasingly international and often younger, rowdier crowd, and some areas are, at times, insalubrious. This also applies to Trastevere, also popular with visitors, late at night.

Try heading to other neighborhoods, such as Testaccio, Ostiense and Pigneto. The first two lie south of the city center (get there by bus or taxi) and have excellent restaurants and great clubs—there's a cluster around Monte Testaccio. The Pigneto district, east of the Lateran and noted for its cutting-edge

---

SUMMER IN THE CITY

Rome's warm summer evenings are conducive to eating and drinking under the stars or strolling to Piazza San Pietro, the Trevi Fountain, Spanish Steps or Colosseum to people-watch and admire the floodlit monuments. The old Ghetto area is charming after dark, and the Pincio, beyond the Spanish Steps, is a great place to watch the sunset. Festivals take place in the city year-round (visit 060608.it), but early June to the end of September sees one of the biggest, the Estate Romana (estateromana. comune.roma.it), with many free events.

Clockwise from top: Taking an evening stroll around Piazza della Rotonda; St. Peter's at dusk; top-quality performers can be heard at classical music events;

street art, is more alternative, with good eating and clubs; you can reach here by tram from Termini to Via Prenestina.

The Musical World

The Auditorium Parco della Musica (▷ 133), Rome's much-loved main performance space, is rightly celebrated for its eclectic program of classical and other music. The city also has a plethora of small musical associations that organize chamber music and other concerts, often in historic settings, such as the Palazzo Doria Pamphilj (▷ 38). Opera in the city, while not as elevated as in Milan or Naples, also benefits from striking settings, notably the Teatro dell'Opera di Roma (▷ 137) and the outdoor Terme di Caracalla (▷ 77). Churches host musical events, not least Sant'Anselmo on the Aventino (▷ 66), where the monks often chant Gregorian plainsong nightly at 7.15.

The Night is Free

Plenty of Rome's nightlife and entertainment costs nothing. Church recitals are often free, and some clubs charge nothing, or next to nothing, during the week. Taking an *aperitivo* is increasingly popular, and many bars offer extensive free snacks with an early evening drink. Festivals throughout the year often have free events, especially those organized by the city council, the Comune di Roma.

NEED TO KNOW

Entry to clubs during the week is usually free, but on weekends you'll pay an entrance fee and may have to buy a *tessera* (temporary membership). Many dance clubs close for the summer, or move to outdoor venues on the coast at, or near, Ostia. For information on nightlife and cultural events, ask hotel concierges, look for fliers, consult *Trovaroma* (a listings magazine free with Thursday's *La Repubblica* newspaper), pick up *Roma Cè* (in shops and bars) or go online at 060608.it or trova-roma.com.

---

enjoy a night of live jazz at a club; there are plenty of bars and clubs to choose from in the city center; early-evening cocktails are a popular start to the night

Directory

Entertainment A–Z

AKAB-CAVE

In the lively Testaccio area, this popular and long-established club is on two levels with a garden area and varied music. Live rock bands and international DJs preside.
⊞ Off map at G9 ⊠ Via di Monte Testaccio 68–69 ☎ 06 5725 0585 🕓 Thu–Sat 11pm–4.30am 🚇 Piramide 🚌 83, 170, 781 to Piazza di Porta San Paolo or Via Monte Testaccio 💶 Expensive

L'ALIBI

This long-established venue has been pulling in clubbers, drawn to its themed evenings and eclectic music blends, for many years. Although considered one of

Rome's best LGBTQ+ clubs, it welcomes everyone to its low-ceilinged dance spaces and fabulous terrace bar, which doubles up as a dance floor during the hot summer months.
⊞ Off map at G9 ⊠ Via di Monte Testaccio 44 ☎ 331 457 0243 🕓 Fri–Sun 11.30pm–4am 🚇 Piramide 🚌 83, 170, 781 to Porta San Paolo or Via di Monte Testaccio 💶 Expensive (includes first drink)

AUDITORIUM CONCILIAZIONE

auditoriumconciliazione.it
There's a wide range of entertainment at this large auditorium on the main road approaching the Vatican. Check out the program

ENTERTAINMENT

of classical and contemporary concerts, theater, dance and film screenings. There's a bar and restaurant, and an art space with changing exhibitions.

🔁 D4 ✉ Via della Conciliazione 4 ☎ 06 683 2256 ⏺ Check for performance times 🚇 Piazza Pia 🚌 23, 32, 49, 492, 994 💵 Moderate

AUDITORIUM PARCO DELLA MUSICA

auditorium.com

This splendid addition to Rome's classical and contemporary music scene, designed by Renzo Piano, has three concert halls in the shape of enormous gray pods set around a vast open-air arena.

🔁 Off map at F1 ✉ Viale Pietro de Coubertin 30 ☎ Infoline 06 8024 1281. Ticket office 892101 (from Italy only, toll line) 🚇 Flaminio then tram 2 🚌 53, 168, 910, 982 💵 Moderate

BAR SAN CALISTO

Bohemian and vibrant San Calisto is where the locals tend to hang out. The piazza-side tables give a window on the real Trastevere and cheap prices make it a great spot to linger. The chocolate, hot with cream in winter and cooling as a *gelato* in summer, is among Rome's best.

🔁 E7 ✉ Piazza di San Calisto 3 ☎ 06 583 5869 ⏺ Mon–Sat 6am–2am 🚌 H, 8 to Viale di Trastevere

BIG BANG

bigbangroma.org

Testaccio was the center of Rome's slaughter industry, and Big Bang, Rome's favorite reggae club, struts its stuff in a graffiti-sprayed former slaughterhouse. Friday night is Bababoomtime night.

🔁 Off map at G9 ✉ Via di Monte Testaccio 22 ☎ 06 6618 3445 ⏺ Fri–Sat 10pm–4.30am 🚇 Piramide 🚌 23, 44, 170, 280 to Via di Monte Testaccio 💵 Expensive

BIG MAMA

bigmama.it

Big Mama's been around a long time, and still draws the crowds to its low-ceilinged basement space in Trastevere. Locals consider it Rome's best blues club, so come here for mellow sounds or pick a night when the accent is on jazz, soul or R and B. It's a very popular place so call in advance if you want to book a table.

🔁 F8 ✉ Vicolo San Francesco a Ripa 18 ☎ 06 581 2551 ⏺ Mid-Sep to Jun Tue–Sat 9pm–1.30am 🚌 H, 8 to Viale di Trastevere 💵 Membership (moderate)

BIG STAR

Tucked away from Trastevere's main action, this gem of a bar-cum-club has a devoted following of Italian and international fans.

🔁 E8 ✉ Via Mameli 25 ☎ 06 581 2479 ⏺ Daily 7.30pm–2.30am 🚇 Piramide 🚌 H, 8, 23, 125, 630, 780 💵 Moderate

CABALA

Located just north of Piazza Navona, Cabala occupies three floors of an historic medieval building, with a piano bar, restaurant and club, plus a terrace with a glorious view over the Tiber. It is intimate and exclusive, so be sure to dress up. Booking a table is recommended. The minimum age for entry is 25.

🔁 F4 ✉ Via dei Soldati 25, near corner of Via dell'Orso ☎ 327 639 8956 ⏺ Fri–Sat 11.30pm–4am 🚌 C3, 70, 81, 87 to Via Zanardelli

CO.SO.

This tiny, stylish, state-of-the-art bar, with its glass shelves of back-lit bottles, is a perfect example of what Pigneto nightlife is all about—laid-back, sharply elegant, cutting edge. It buzzes nightly with people, who come to sample the eclectic cocktails and mixed drinks.

🌐 Off map at M8 ✉ Via Braccia da Montone 80 ☎ 06 4543 5428 🕙 Mon–Sat 6.30pm–2am 🚌 81, 150, 412, 810, tram 5, 14, 19

CUL DE SAC

enotecaculdesacroma.it
Rome's original informal wine bar, near Piazza Navona, has pine tables and a big marble bar. More than 1,400 wines are on offer, plus snacks, light meals and cheese and salami from every region in Italy.

🌐 F5 ✉ Piazza Pasquino 73 ☎ 06 6880 1094 🕙 Daily 12–12 🚌 46, 62, 64 to Corso Vittorio Emanuele II

DRUID'S DEN

druidspubrome.com
This friendly Irish pub appeals to Romans and expats alike. Also try the Fiddler's Elbow, a popular sister pub around the corner at Via dell'Olmata 43.

🌐 K6 ✉ Via San Martino ai Monti 28 ☎ 06 4890 4781 🕙 Daily 5pm–2am 🚇 Cavour 🚌 75, 117 to Via Cavour or 16, 70, 71, 360 to Piazza Santa Maria Maggiore

ENOTECA TRASTEVERE

enotecatrastevere.it
Shelves groaning with bottles line the brick walls of this very popular wine bar in the heart of Trastevere. You will find more than 900 wines to choose from, mainly Italian, plus a weekly selection of reds and whites available by the glass or bottle. You can eat a light meal too, and weekends bring live piano music. Tables spill outside during the summer.

🌐 F7 ✉ Via della Lungaretta 86 ☎ 06 588 5659 🕙 Daily noon–2am 🚌 H, 8, 780 to Piazza Sidney Sonnino

ESCOPAZZO

escopazzo.it
This intimate bar, with its warm wood and sleek steel decor, lies just off Piazza Venezia and offers DJ sets several nights a week. There's occasional live music, while Thursday evenings draw the crowds for karaoke night. It's also popular for private parties, so check ahead for what's happening on the evening you choose to visit.

🌐 G6 ✉ Via d'Aracoeli 41 ☎ 389 683 5618 🕙 Daily 10am–3am 🚌 40, 64, 170 and other services to Piazza Venezia

ETABLI

etabli.it
Open all hours, Etabli is a real find, a welcoming, relaxed bar-lounge-restaurant that's housed in a 16th-century palazzo just west of Piazza Navona. Sit at a scrubbed wooden table or sink into a leather armchair for breakfast, brunch, tea or dinner—or simply pop in for a drink. The menu offers well-sourced cheeses and *salumi*, there's home baking and a great range of fresh juices and smoothies, as well as every imaginable type of alcohol.

🌐 E5 ✉ Vicolo delle Vacche 9a ☎ 06 9761 6694 🕙 Mon–Sat 7am–1.30am, Sun 9am–1am 🚌 46, 62, 64 to Corso Vittorio Emanuele II

FRENI E FRIZIONI

freniefrizioni.com

At the heart of Trastevere, this sleek, modern bar offers the chance to drink and eat light meals either in the pared-down interior or outside in the small piazza.

🔲 E7 ✉ Via del Politeama 4–6 ☎ 06 4549 7499 🕐 Daily 6.30pm–2am 🚍 H, 8 to Viale di Trastevere

A great spot for an evening drink

LANIFICIO 159

lanificio159.com

Once a wool factory, this ex-industrial complex in Rome's northeastern suburbs is now home to a multi-purpose venue. It hosts exhibitions, art and photography shows, Sunday markets and work-shops, while its underground club space is given over to live gigs and DJ sets by top Roman and international crews.

🔲 Off map at M1 ✉ Via Pietralata 159a ☎ 06 4178 0081 🕐 Restaurant daily 12.30–3, 7.30–10.30; exhibition space varies; club usually Thu–Sat 11pm–4am 🚇 Pietralata

NUOVO SACHER

sacherfilm.eu

Although dedicated to Italian film talent, this cinema occasionally shows foreign films in *versione originale* on Monday. It seats up to 360 people; in summer there are screenings in the courtyard.

🔲 F8 ✉ Largo Ascianghi 1 ☎ 06 581 8116 🕐 Daily 4–10 🚍 H, 8 to Viale di Trastevere 🎟 Moderate

OMBRE ROSSE

ombrerosseintrastevere.it

This is a friendly, intimate all-day and late-night bar in the heart of Trastevere, with walls covered in music and movie posters, outdoor seating and live music most nights. There's a limited menu of soups, pastas and light meals.

🔲 E7 ✉ Piazza Sant'Egidio 12–13 ☎ 06 588 4155 🕐 Daily 10am–2am 🚍 H, 8, 780 to Viale di Trastevere

OPPIO CAFFÈ

oppiocaffe.it

Old, vaulted brick walls are offset by contemporary fittings in this airy café-bar-club on the street just north of the Colosseum, by Colle Oppio park. There are wonderful floodlit views of the amphitheater plus live music some nights, and DJs most Fridays and Saturdays.

🔲 J7 ✉ Via delle Terme di Tito 72 ☎ 06 474 5262 🕐 Daily 7am–2am; closed in Aug 🚇 Colosseo 🚍 C3, 3, 51, 85, 87, 117 to Piazza del Colosseo

---

MUSIC OUTDOORS

Alfresco recitals often take place throughout the city in summer. Locations include the cloisters of Santa Maria della Pace; the Villa Doria Pamphilj; the grounds of the Villa Giulia; and the Area Archeologica del Teatro di Marcello from July to September (as part of the Estate al Tempietto, also known as the Concerti del Tempietto, tempietto.it). Venues are subject to change.

Enjoy an evening of classical music

RADIO LONDRA

radiolondradiscobar.com

Clubbers love this cave-like venue, heaving with an international and local crowd. It's jam-packed on weekends, when its fans come to enjoy the retro-house, rock and funk and the friendly vibe.

🞢 Off map at G9 ✉ Via di Monte Testaccio 67 ☎ 06 574 7904 ⏲ Wed–Mon 11pm–4.30am 🚇 Piramide 🚌 83, 170, 781 to Porta San Paolo or Via Monte Testaccio 💶 Moderate

RIPA PLACE

worldhotelriparoma.com

This stylish café and lounge is part of the four-star Worldhotel Ripa Roma, located in a quiet spot near the Tiber between Via Portuense and Viale di Trastevere. It's a great choice for an early cocktail or aperitif.

🞢 E9 ✉ Via degli Orti di Trastevere 1 ☎ 06 58611 ⏲ Bar-café 10.30am– 11.30pm, restaurant 12.30–2.30, 7.30–11 🚌 H, 8 to Viale di Trastevere

SALOTTO 42

salotto42.it

Sleek design and great comfort give this stylish all-day haunt on lovely Piazza di Pietro something special. You can relax here, have a drink and graze during the day and enjoy cocktails and the superb sound system in the evenings.

🞢 G5 ✉ Piazza di Pietro 42 ☎ 06 678 5804 ⏲ Tue–Sat 10am–2am, Sun–Mon 10am–midnight 🚌 C3, 51, 62, 63, 80, 117 to Via del Corso

SILVANO TOTI GLOBE THEATRE

globetheatreroma.com

This replica Elizabethan theater is modeled on London's Globe. Unlike London, weather is not normally a problem, and you can take in Shakespeare's work under the stars in Italian or, sometimes, English.

🞢 H2 ✉ Largo Aqua Felix, Villa Borghese ☎ 060608 🚌 C3, 53

STADIO OLIMPICO

Football teams AS Roma and Lazio are based here. Games are played on alternate Sundays.

🞢 Off map at C1 ✉ Via del Foro Italico ☎ 06 323 7333 (box office) or 06 36851 🚇 Ottaviano, then bus 32 to Piazzale della Farnesina/Stadio Tennis

---

APERITIVO TIME

The great Torinese predilection for the pre-dinner *aperitivo* has arrived in Rome. Arrive in many bars after 7pm and you can feast or graze on generous snacks of pasta, cold meats, couscous, cheese and much more, all for the price of a glass of wine. Popular *aperitivo* bars are opening all the time. You'll find these bars throughout the historic core, particularly around Piazza Navona, and in Trastevere.

AS Roma information:
Tickets (non-transferable) are available online and at many outlets around Rome. Photo ID is required to enter the stadium. Full list of sellers on asroma.com. Also from Lottomatica stores and AS Roma outlets (✉ Piazza Colonna 360 ☎ 06 8938 6000)

Lazio information:
Tickets can be bought online at sslazio.it. Also at Lottomatica stores or authorized outlets (details at sslazio.it) ☎ 06 9760 7111

STRAVINSKIJ BAR

roccofortehotels.com
Picasso and the writer Jean Cocteau whiled away hours in these gardens, now the setting for a pretty, if expensive, hotel bar.
✚ G3 ✉ Hotel de Russie, Via del Babuino 9 ☎ 06 328 881 🕐 Daily 9am–1am 🚇 Flaminio 🚌 117

TEATRO OLIMPICO

teatroolimpico.it
The Filarmonica di Roma performs here, as well as other international dance and music ensembles.
✚ Off map at F1 ✉ Piazza Gentile da Fabriano 17 ☎ Box Office 06 326 5991 🚌 910 to Pannini or metro A to Flaminio, then tram 2 to Piazza Mancini

TEATRO DELL'OPERA DI ROMA

operaroma.it
One of Italy's top opera houses is also an official venue for ballet. Summer performances are staged outdoors in the Terme di Caracalla. The spacious foyer displays a permanent exhibition of artworks and costumes owned by the Opera House.
✚ J–K5 ✉ Piazza Beniamino Gigli 1 ☎ 06 481 601/06 488 1755 🚇 Termini 🚌 H, 40, 60, 64, 70, 71, 170 to Via Nazionale or services to Termini

TEATRO VASCELLO

teatrovascello.it
On the edge of Trastevere, this is a small but good venue for experimental dance. It also hosts classical ballet, multimedia events and children's shows.
✚ D8 ✉ Via Giacinto Carini 78 ☎ 06 589 8031 🕐 Sep–Jun Tue–Sat 5.30–9, Sun 3–5 🚌 44, 75, 710, 870

Wine bar in Trastevere

ENTERTAINMENT

Eat

There are places to eat across the city to suit all tastes and budgets. In this section, establishments are listed alphabetically.

EAT

Introduction

Eating in Rome is utter pleasure, whether it's grabbing a slice of pizza to go, lingering over a long alfresco lunch or tucking into traditional favorites at a family-run trattoria. With so much choice, deciding where to eat will be one of the most enjoyable parts of your Roman experience.

What to Eat

Rome's restaurant scene is thriving, with top restaurants becoming more sophisticated and stressing *cucina creativa*—creative cooking. The majority are still family-run, with the accent on local dishes. The classics here are robust and filling; pasta, including the iconic *spaghetti alla carbonara* (with egg and lardons), meat dishes using offal (brains, liver and tripe), salt cod, veal and pork. Wines are unpretentious and include Frascati from the Alban Hills south of the city.

Where to Eat

Central Rome's restaurants are concentrated in the streets around Piazza Navona and the Pantheon. Trastevere is also a traditional dining area, along with the more outlying Testaccio, Pigneto and San Lorenzo. Romans demand value for money, resulting in the return of traditional *trattorie* and *osterie*, plus the emergence of informal wine bars *(enoteche)*, salad bars and Italian-style diners. The food may often be simple, but culinary standards are usually high.

CUTTING COSTS

In bars, you will pay less for food and drink if you stand at the bar rather than sitting at waiter-service tables. Most have a selection of rolls *(panini)* and sandwiches *(tramezzini)*. For tap rather than bottled water, ask for *acqua dal rubinetto, per favore*. Pizza by the slice makes a good lunchtime snack—tiny establishments can be found across the city: look for signs "Pizza al Taglio" or "Pizza al Forno." Many *alimentari* (small food shops) will make up a round Roman roll *(una rosetta)* with cheese or ham.

From top: Pizza and pasta are available everywhere; visit a deli for delicious bread for a picnic; start the day with a cappuccino

Directory

THE ANCIENT CITY
Coffee/Pastries
Antico Caffè del Brasile
Fine Dining
Antonello Colonna Open
Gelaterie
Torcè
Roman/Italian
Il Bocconcino
Pasqualino al Colosseo
Silvio alla Suburra

CENTRAL ROME
Coffee/Pastries
Bar del Fico
La Caffettiera
Sant'Eustachio
La Tazza d'Oro
Fine Dining
Il Convivio Troiani
Il Pagliaccio
Gelaterie
Gelateria della Palma
Tre Scalini
Pizza/Pasta
Da Baffetto
Roman/Italian
Antica Birreria Peroni
Armando al Pantheon
Le Cave di Sant'Ignazio
Da Francesco
Ditirambo
Grano
'Gusto
Maccheroni
Supplizio
World Cuisines
L'Eau Vive

TRASTEVERE AND THE SOUTH
Fine Dining
Checchino dal 1887
Glass Hostaria
Gelateria
Alberto Pica

Pizza/Pasta
Dar Poeta
Ivo
Panattoni Ai Marmi
Roman/Italian
L'Arcangelo
Casetta de' Trastevere
Checco er Carettiere
Da Augusto
Da Felice
Giggetto
Piperno
Sora Lella
Vecchia Roma

NORTHERN ROME
Gelaterie
Il Gelato di San Crispino
Roman/Italian
Matricianella
Vegetarian
Margutta RistorArte

VATICAN AND AROUND
Pizza/Pasta
Pizzarium Bonci
La Pratolina
Roman/Italian
Dal Toscano
Del Frate

FARTHER AFIELD
Bars by Day
Bar Necci dal 1924
Roman/Italian
Cacciani
Priscilla
Ristorante Sibilla
Zarazà

Eating A–Z

EAT

PRICES

Prices are approximate, based on a 3-course meal for one person.

€€€	over €60
€€	€40–€60
€	under €40

ALBERTO PICA €

Alberto Pica offers around 20 different varieties of excellent ice cream; try one of their specialties such as pistachio, green apple (mele verde) or Sicilian citrus (agrumi di Sicilia).

🔲 F6 ✉ Via della Seggiola 12 ☎ 06 686 8405 🕐 Daily 8am–midnight, longer hours in summer; closed 2 weeks in Aug 🚌 8 to Via Arenula and 46, 62, 64, 70, 81, 87, 492 to Largo di Torre Argentina

ANTICA BIRRERIA PERONI €

anticabirreriaperoni.net

Generations of both Romans and tourists have packed this beer hall for years, quenching their thirst with draft Peroni or one of the other tap beers on offer. Food is straightforward and hearty, with daily changing pasta and meat dishes and a few salads. You can eat standing at the bar if you're pressed for time.

🔲 G5 ✉ Via di San Marcello 19 ☎ 06 679 5310 🕐 Mon–Sat 12–12 🚌 63, 81, 87 and all other buses to Piazza Venezia

ANTICO CAFFÈ DEL BRASILE €

A superb variety of beans and ground coffee is sold from huge sacks or at the bar. John Paul II bought his coffee here before his pontificate—try the "Pope's blend."

🔲 J6 ✉ Via dei Serpenti 23 ☎ 06 488 2319 🕐 Mon–Sat 6am-8.30pm, Sun 7am–8pm; closed Sat from 2pm and Sun Jun–Aug 🚌 60, 64, 70, 170 to Via Nazionale or 75, 117 to Via Cavour

ANTONELLO COLONNA OPEN €€–€€€

antonellocolonna.it

Celebrated chef Antonello Colonna has earned Michelin stars for his sophisticated cooking in this futuristic, virtually all-glass restaurant in the Palazzo delle Esposizioni. Go for the good-value City Lunch from Tuesday to Friday (choose from an all-you-can-eat buffet at €18) or for brunch at weekends for €30.

🔲 H5 ✉ Via Milano 9a, corner of Via Nazionale ☎ 06 4782 2641 🕐 Tue–Sat 12.30–3.30, 7–10.30, Sun 12.30–3.30 🚌 40, 60, 64, 70, 170 and services to Via Nazionale

L'ARCANGELO €€€

larcangelo.com

The wood paneling, black and white photographs and leather banquettes add to the traditional charm of this restaurant. Founded, in fact, within the last 25 years, it is not as venerable as it seems and

THE MENU

Starters are called antipasti; first course (soup, pasta or risotto) is il primo; and main meat and fish dishes are il secondo. Salads (insalata) and vegetables (contorni) are ordered (and often eaten) separately. Desserts are dolci, with cheese (formaggio) or fruit (frutta) to follow. If no menu card is offered, ask for la lista or il menù. A set-price menu (un menù turistico) may seem good value, but portions are usually small and the food is invariably poor—usually just spaghetti with a tomato sauce, followed by a piece of chicken and fruit.

one of the first of Rome's eating places to update the traditional trattoria formula. The food is excellent, with new twists on old favorites.

➕ E3 ✉ Via Giuseppe Gioacchino Belli 59 ☎ 06 321 0992 🕐 Mon–Fri 1–2.30, 8–11, Sat 8–11pm 🚇 Lepanto 🚌 30, 49, 70, 87, 130, 990 to Piazza Cavour or Via Cicerone

ARMANDO AL PANTHEON €€

armandoalpantheon.it

Armando's welcoming family has been cooking Roman classics for generations in this wonderfully traditional restaurant in the heart of the *centro storico*, moments from the Pantheon. All the great Roman classic specialties are on the menu, making this one of the best places to enjoy dishes such as *spaghetti alla matriciana* (with spicy ham and tomato), *cacio e pepe* (with sheep's cheese and black pepper) or *saltimbocca alla romana* (veal with sage and ham). Booking is essential.

➕ F5 ✉ Salita dei Crescenzi 31 ☎ 06 6880 3034 🕐 Mon–Fri 12.30–3, 7–11, Sat 12.30–3 (closed Aug) 🚌 40, 64, 70 and other services to Largo Torre di Argentina

BAR DEL FICO €

bardelfico.com

This simple retreat just west of Piazza Navona has been a reliable city-center fixture for decades. Visit for a morning coffee (there are tables inside or out), join Rome's younger crowd at the bar for aperitifs, or try the restaurant for good, straightforward food such as pizza, pasta and gourmet burgers.

➕ E5 ✉ Piazza del Fico 26–28/Via della Pace 34–35 ☎ 06 6889 1373 🕐 Daily 8am–2am 🚌 40, 46, 62, 64 on Corso Vittorio Emanuele II to Chiesa Nuova

Dining in style

BAR NECCI DAL 1924 €–€€

necci1924.com

This all-day bar-restaurant was one of the first that helped put Pigneto on the map. Come here for anything from breakfast to dinner or just for a drink, and enjoy the fresh, seasonal cooking. The easiest access is by taxi or metro after a visit to San Giovanni in Laterano.

➕ Off map at M8 ✉ Via Fanfulla da Lodi 68 ☎ 06 9760 1552 🕐 Daily 8am–1am 🚇 Pigneto 🚌 16, 51, 81, 85

IL BOCCONCINO €

ilbocconcino.com

A recent but traditional-looking trattoria, Bocconcino offers classic Roman dishes, though service may be slow at busy times. It is one of several good options in the streets east of the Colosseum—also try Café Café around the corner at Via dei SS Quattro 44 for snacks and light lunches, or Luzzi (closed Wed), at Via San Giovanni in Laterano 88, for pizzas.

➕ J7 ✉ Via Ostilia 23 ☎ 06 7707 9175 🕐 Thu–Tue 12.30–3.30, 7.30–11; closed 2 weeks in Aug 🚇 Colosseo 🚌 All services to the Colosseum

EAT

Traditional pizzas at Da Baffetto

CACCIANI €€
cacciani.it
This established hotel restaurant in the heart of Frascati serves Roman and classic Italian dishes. Try the house specialty, *pollo alla romana* (whole chicken cooked in a tomato and bell pepper sauce).
✉ Via Armando Diaz 13, Frascati ☎ 06 940 1991 🕐 Tue–Sun 12.30–2.30, 7–10.30; closed Sun evening Oct–May, and Jan 7–14, Aug 16–26

LA CAFFETTIERA €
lacaffettieraroma.it
Great coffee, light meals and mouthwatering pastries and cakes are the order of the day at this bar/tearoom.
➕ G5 ✉ Piazza di Pietro 65 ☎ 06 679 8147 🕐 Daily 7.30am–9pm 🚌 C3, 51, 62, 63, 80, 117 to Via del Corso

CASETTA DE' TRASTEVERE
€–€€
This curious restaurant at the heart of Trastevere has tables outside on a quiet square. The appealing interior recreates a traditional Roman piazza, complete with balconied houses. Expect straight-forward Roman cooking.
➕ E7 ✉ Piazza de' Renzi 31a–32 ☎ 06 580 0158 🕐 Daily 12–12 🚌 23, 125, 280 to Ponte Sisto–Piazza Trilussa

LE CAVE DI SANT'IGNAZIO €
dasabatino.it
Also known as Da Sabatino, this restaurant is part of a dying breed of simple, low-cost, family-run central Roman trattorias. Inside there are several dining rooms, plus tables outside on the pretty and intimate little Piazza Sant'Ignazio. The Roman wine and food are unpretentious—pizzas from a wood-fired oven, for exam-ple, or cheese and black pepper *cacio e pepe* pasta; the *antipasti* are a meal in themselves.
➕ G5 ✉ Piazza Sant'Ignazio 169, off Via del Seminario ☎ 06 679 7821 🕐 Daily 12.30–3.30, 6.30–midnight 🚌 C3, 51, 62, 63, 80, 83, 85 to Via del Corso

CHECCHINO DAL 1887 €€€
checchino-dal-1887.com
Robust appetites are required for the menu at this Testaccio estab-lishment. Quintessential Roman dishes relying largely on offal are

EAT

the specialty. There is outdoor seating during the summer. Reservations are advisable.

🔲 Off map at G9 ⊠ Via Monte Testaccio 30 ☎ 06 574 3816 🕒 Tue–Sat 12.30–3, 8–11; closed Aug, Dec 24–Jan 2 🚌 3, 75, 118 to Piramide

CHECCO ER CARETTIERE €€–€€€

checcoercarettiere.it

This Trastevere beacon to traditional cooking is adorned with black-and-white celebrity photos. Good seafood and homemade specialties dominate the menu, while a patio and internal garden room cater to smokers.

🔲 E7 ⊠ Via Benedetta, 10–13 ☎ 06 581 7018 🕒 Daily 12–3, 7.30–midnight 🚌 23, 125, 280 to Piazza Trilussa

IL CONVIVIO TROIANI €€€

ilconviviotroiani.com

The Troiani brothers from the Marche region have created a tranquil little restaurant with a reputation for innovative and subtle modern dishes.

🔲 F4 ⊠ Vicolo dei Soldati 31 ☎ 06 686 9432 🕒 Mon–Sat dinner only 8–11pm; closed Aug 13–17 🚌 30, 70, 81, 87, 130, 492 to Corso del Rinascimento

DA AUGUSTO €

Packed with locals and set on one of Trastevere's prettiest squares, this time-warp family restaurant is a window on traditional Roman eating out. Delicious homestyle cooking, huge portions and classic Roman dishes are the key notes—expect to see plenty of rabbit, offal and filling pasta on the menu—while the basic decor provides a suitable backdrop to the experience. Payment is by cash only.

🔲 E7 ⊠ Piazza de' Renzi 15 ☎ 06 580 3798 🕒 Daily 12.30–3, 8–11 🚌 H, 8, 23, 125, 280, 780

DA BAFFETTO €

pizzeriabaffetto.it

This tiny, hole-in-the-wall pizzeria has retained its atmosphere and low prices. Thin, crisp pizzas fired in a traditional oven are the specialty, with all the classic toppings, including a spicy sausage and onion and mozzarella and zucchini flowers. It's very popular so expect to wait for a table.

🔲 E5 ⊠ Via del Governo Vecchio 114 ☎ 06 686 1617 🕒 Daily 6.30pm–1am; closed Aug 🚌 46, 62, 64 to Corso Vittorio Emanuele II

DA FELICE €€

felicetestaccio.it

The Trivelloni family has run this Testaccio restaurant since 1936, serving generations of diners with Roman classic dishes. You can expect typical ingredients such as artichokes, beans, lentils, spelt, offal, boiled meat and chicken—all seasonal. Specials change daily and this generation of the family have turned the place into one of

EAT

TIME TO PAY

The bill (check), *il conto*, usually includes extras such as *servizio* (service). Iniquitous cover charges (*pane e coperto*) have now been outlawed, but some restaurants still try to get round the regulations. Only pay for bread (*pane*) if you have asked for it. Proper receipts—not a scrawled piece of paper—must be given by law. If you receive a scrap of paper, which is more likely in a pizzeria, and have doubts about the total, be sure to ask for a proper receipt (*una fattura* or *una ricevuta*).

Rome's most buzzing eating choices. Booking is essential.
🚇 Off map at G9 ✉ Via Mastro Giorgio 29, Testaccio ☎ 06 574 6800 🕐 Daily 12.30–3, 8–11.30; closed 3 weeks in Aug 🚇 Piramide 🚌 3, 23, 30, 75, 130, 280 to Via Marmorata

DA FRANCESCO €

dafrancesco.it
This simple restaurant near Piazza Navona has never lost its appeal over the years, thanks to a warm, friendly atmosphere, good Roman food and low prices. There are no reservations, so arrive early.
🚇 E5 ✉ Piazza del Fico 29 ☎ 06 686 4009 🕐 Daily 12–3.30, 7–12.30 🚌 64 and other services to Chiesa Nuova on Corso Vittorio Emanuele II

DAL TOSCANO €–€€

This large trattoria north of Piazza San Pietro serves Tuscan food, and is particularly known for its meats and its wood-fired grill. You'll also find the thick vegetable soups *(ribollita)*, stews and bean dishes so popular in Tuscany.
🚇 C3 ✉ Via Germanico 58/60 ☎ 06 3972 5717 🕐 Tue–Sun 12.30–3, 8–11.15 🚇 Ottaviano 🚌 19, 23, 32, 49, 492 to Piazza del Risorgimento

DAR POETA €

darpoeta.com
A popular pizzeria hidden in a quiet street, Dar Poeta has a simple interior (plus a few outdoor tables), but the thin pizzas and desserts are creative and excellent.
🚇 E7 ✉ Vicolo di Bologna 45 ☎ 06 588 0516 🕐 Daily 12–11 🚌 H, 8, 870 and all services to Trastevere

DEL FRATE €€

enotecadelfrate.it
This attractive, sleek wine bar is just a few minutes' walk from the Vatican Museums. The wine list is superb, with many interesting wines on offer by the glass, and the menu modern, imaginative and lighter than those in many Roman eating houses. The cheese list features regional specialties from all over Italy.
🚇 D3 ✉ Via degli Scipioni 118–122 ☎ 06 323 6437 🕐 Tue–Fri 12–3, 8–11.45, Sat, Mon 8–11.45pm 🚇 Ottaviano 🚌 23, 49, 492 to Piazza del Risorgimento or 19, 32, 49, 70 to Viale Giulio Cesare

DITIRAMBO €€

ristoranteditirambo.it
The kitchen in this small restaurant uses organic ingredients, as well as producing homemade bread, pasta and desserts. Expect Italian cooking with a creative twist. Reservations are essential.
🚇 F6 ✉ Piazza della Cancelleria 75 ☎ 06 687 1626 🕐 Tue–Sun 12.45–3.15, 7.30–11.30, Mon 7pm–11.30pm; closed part of Aug 🚌 46, 62, 64 to Corso Vittorio Emanuele II

EAT

L'EAU VIVE €€

eauvive.it

The menu here is predominantly French, with dishes such as guinea fowl, classic salads and foie gras, and a daily special that's a French take on international cuisine. The dining rooms are elegant, and it's excellent value—there are lunch menus at €10, €14 and €18. You will be served by nuns (▷ panel, 144).

🚇 F5 ✉ Via Monterone 85 🕐 Mon–Sat 12.30–2.30, 7–10.30; closed Aug 🚌 8, 46, 62, 64, 70, 87, 492 to Largo di Torre Argentina

GELATERIA DELLA PALMA €

dellapalma.it

Choose from more than 100 varieties of ice cream at this big, brash place near the Trevi Fountain. It also offers cakes and chocolates.

🚇 F5 ✉ Via della Maddalena 20 ☎ 06 6880 6752 🕐 Daily 8.30am–midnight or later 🚌 All services to Via del Corso or Corso del Rinascimento

IL GELATO DI SAN CRISPINO €

ilgelatodisancrispino.com

Come here for the delicious ice cream. There's a second outlet at Piazza Maddalena 3 (daily 11am–12.30am, closed Tue Oct–Mar), just north of the Pantheon.

🚇 H4 ✉ Via della Panetteria 42 ☎ 06 679 3924 🕐 Sun–Thu 11am–12.30am, Fri–Sat 11am–1.30am 🚇 Barberini

GIGGETTO €

giggetto.it

This famous Romano-Jewish restaurant in the Ghetto district has been in business for over 80 years. Try the classic *carciofi alla giudea* (Jewish-style artichokes).

🚇 G6 ✉ Via Portico d'Ottavia 21a ☎ 06 686 1105 🕐 Tue–Sun 12.30–3, 7.30–11; closed late Jul, Aug 🚌 H, 8, 63 to Via Arenula and 46, 62, 70 and other services to Largo di Torre Argentina

GLASS HOSTARIA €€€

glasshostaria.it

The contemporary styling of this striking restaurant is a world away from that of the traditional Roman trattoria. The ultra-modern design is matched by excellent, creative Italian cooking that earned a Michelin star in 2011. Try one of the the special menus—tasting, veggie or traditional.

🚇 E7 ✉ Vicolo del Cinque 58 ☎ 06 5833 5903 🕐 Tue–Sun 7.30pm–11.30pm 🚌 23, 125, 280 to Ponte Sisto–Piazza Trilussa

GRANO €€

ristorantegrano.it

Whether you love or hate the virtually all-white decor of this faux-rustic bar and restaurant, the innovative southern Italian cooking is excellent.

🚇 F5 ✉ Piazza Rondanini 53 ☎ 06 6819 2096 🕐 Daily 12.30–3, 7.30–12 🚌 30, 70, 81, 87 and other services to Corso del Risorgimento

---

BUYING ICE CREAM

Ice cream *(gelato)* in a proper *gelateria* (ice cream shop) is sold either in a cone *(un cono)* or a paper cup *(una coppa)*. Specify which you want and then decide how much you wish to pay. Sizes of cone and cup go up in price bands, usually starting small and ending enormous. You can select up to two or three varieties (more in bigger tubs) and will usually be asked if you want a swirl of cream *(panna)* to round things off.

'GUSTO €€

gusto.it

This chic, modern restaurant spreads over two levels where you can eat pizzas, salads and other light meals downstairs or fuller meals upstairs. There is also a bookstore and kitchenware shop.

🔲 F3 ✉ Piazza Augusto Imperatore 9 ☎ 06 6813 4221 🕔 Daily 12.30pm–12.30am 🚌 117 to Via del Corso

IVO €

ivoatrastevere.it

Lines are common at Trastevere's best-known pizzeria, but turnover is quick, so it's worth waiting for these thin, crisp *pizze* with both classic and adventurous toppings.

🔲 E7 ✉ Via di San Francesco a Ripa 158 ☎ 06 581 7082 🕔 Mon, Wed–Sat 6pm–12.30am, Sun 12–4, 6–12.30; closed 3 weeks Aug 🚌 H, 8, 780 to Viale di Trastevere

MACCHERONI €€

risorantemaccheroni.com

This popular, informal restaurant has several attractive, rustic dining rooms plus tables outside on the

A tempting plate of pasta

square; the basement rooms are not as nice. Attentive staff serve good, traditional Italian dishes—it's known for its carbonara.

🔲 F5 ✉ Piazza delle Coppelle 44 ☎ 06 6830 7895 🕔 Daily 12.30–3, 7–11.30 🚌 8, 64, 87 and other services to Largo di Torre Argentina and Via del Corso

MARGUTTA RISTORARTE €–€€

ilmargutta.bio

There are few good vegetarian restaurants in Rome; Margutta is the exception, and good value too. Lunch is served buffet style, with over 50 dishes featuring fresh organic vegetables, as well as pasta and pizza. Expect to pay more in the evenings, when there is sometimes live jazz.

🔲 G3 ✉ Via Margutta 118 ☎ 06 3265 0577 🕔 Daily 12.30–11.30 🚇 Spagna 🚌 117

MATRICIANELLA €€

matricianella.it

This trattoria is close to Via del Corso, not far from the parliament building. It offers Roman cooking with the odd twist and has a few outside tables in summer.

🔲 G4 ✉ Via del Leone 4 ☎ 06 683 2100 🕔 Mon–Sat 12.30–3, 7.30–11; closed Sun and 3 weeks in Aug 🚌 All services to Via del Corso

NONNA BETTA €–€€

nonnabetta.it

You'll find classic Romano-Jewish cuisine at this Ghetto restaurant, which is cozy in winter and spills outside in summer. The menu is strictly kosher so there are two options—meat dishes or fish and dairy; choose one or the other. Pasta is homemade, the artichokes are spot on, and there's enough tripe, sweetbread, liver and brains to please the most ardent carnivore.

🔲 G6 ✉ Via del Portico d'Ottavia 16 ☎ 06 6880 6263 🕙 Wed–Mon 11–11 🚋 H, 3, 8, 63, 70, 87 and other services to Largo di Torre Argentina

IL PAGLIACCIO €€€

ristoranteilpagliaccio.it

Inventive chef Anthony Genovese has won Michelin stars in the past, and this formal gourmet experience continues to be a superb combination of Asian, Mediterranean and traditional Italian cuisine.

🔲 E5 ✉ Via dei Banchi Vecchi 129 ☎ 06 6880 9595 🕙 Wed–Sat 12.30–2, 7.30–10.30; Tue dinner only; closed part Jan, Aug 🚋 40, 46, 62, 64 to Chiesa Nuova on Corso Vittorio Emanuele II

PANATTONI AI MARMI €

Panattoni is known locally as "L'Obitorio" (The Morgue) on account of its characteristic cold marble-topped tables. You can watch the flamboyant chef flip the pizzas at the oven. Arrive early to secure a table outside.

🔲 F8 ✉ Viale di Trastevere 53 ☎ 06 580 0919 🕙 Thu–Tue 6.30pm–2am; closed 3 weeks in Aug 🚋 H, 8, 780 to Viale di Trastevere

PASQUALINO AL COLOSSEO €€

pasqualinoalcolosseo.it

This simple and welcoming long-established trattoria near the Colosseum serves good, robust Roman classics, such as *abbachio* (roast lamb) and *saltimbocca* (veal escalope with prosciutto and sage), pizzas and large main course salads.

🔲 K7 ✉ Via SS. Quattro Coronati 66 ☎ 06 700 4576 🕙 Daily 12–3, 7–11; closed 2 weeks in Aug 🚇 Colosseo 🚋 85, 117 to Via di San Giovanni in Laterano or services to Piazza del Colosseo

PIPERNO €€

ristorantepiperno.com

Much Roman cuisine is based on the city's Jewish culinary traditions. Piperno has been a temple to Romano-Jewish cuisine for over a century. This is a very popular destination, especially for Sunday lunch, so reserve ahead.

🔲 F6 ✉ Via Monte de' Cenci 9 ☎ 06 6880 6629/6833 606 🕙 Tue–Sat 12.45–2.30, 7.45–10.30, Sun 12.45–3; closed Aug 🚋 H, 8, 63 to Via Arenula and 8, 46, 62, 64, 70, 87, 492 to Largo di Torre Argentina

PIZZARIUM BONCI €

bonci.it

You can't sit down in this tiny takeout pizzeria, but you can eat what is considered to be Rome's finest pizza. Master *pizzaiolo* Gabriele Bonci uses organic flour for his dough, then tops the crust with not only classic mixes but inventive flavors of his own.

EAT

A3/B4 ✉ Via della Meloria 43 ☎ 06 3974 5416 🕐 Mon–Sat 11–10, Sun 12–4, 6–10 🚇 Cipro 🚌 49, 490, 492

LA PRATOLINA €

pizzeriaalapratolina.it

Pizzas here are called *pinsa* in homage to their oval shape, a throwback apparently to bread in ancient Rome. The 37 varieties of toppings range from the classic to the innovative. There are also salads, *crocchette* and antipasti.

C3 ✉ Via degli Scipioni 248 ☎ 06 3600 4409 🕐 Mon–Sat 7pm–midnight 🚇 Lepanto/Ottaviano 🚌 30, 70, 81, 87, 130, 280

PRISCILLA €

trattoriapriscilla.it

After a morning exploring the Via Appia Antica, head to this atmospheric traditional restaurant to recharge your batteries. The shortish menu offers Roman classics, freshly prepared, and the desserts are homemade.

Off map at K9 ✉ Via Appia Antica 68 ☎ 06 513 6379 🕐 Mon–Sat 12–3, 7–11.30; closed part of Feb and Aug

RISTORANTE SIBILLA €€€

ristorantesibilla.com

This restaurant enjoys a glorious setting by Tivoli's circular Temple of Vesta. Dishes might include *cannelloni alle tre carni* (cannelloni with a three-meat filling) and *agnello scottaditto con la cicoria* (grilled lamb with chicory), prepared on an open wood stove.

✉ Via della Sibilla 50, Tivoli ☎ 0774 335281 🕐 Tue–Sun 12.30–3, 7.30–10.30

SANT'EUSTACHIO €

santeustachioilcaffe.com

Excellent coffee is served inside and out at one of Rome's best cafés, accompanied by tasty treats. It also sells beans, capsules, ground coffee and coffee-based chocolates for you to take home.

F5 ✉ Piazza Sant'Eustachio 82 ☎ 06 6880 2048 🕐 Daily 8.30am–1am (Sat until 2am) 🚌 30, 70, 81, 87, 130 to Corso del Rinascimento

SILVIO ALLA SUBURRA €

osteriadellasuburra.it

This simple restaurant, also known as Osteria della Suburra, is in a quiet street just a few minutes' walk from the Colosseum. The pastas are homemade and there's a good house wine from the Frascati Hills.

J6 ✉ Via Urbana 67–69 ☎ 06 486 531 🕐 Tue–Sun 12.45–3, 7–11 🚇 Cavour

SORA LELLA €€–€€€

trattoriasoralella.it

Originally founded by the actress Sora Lella, this is a former trattoria on the Isola Tiberina. Enjoy Roman cooking, with seasonal dishes, daily specials and house specialties that have been served for many years. They also offer gluten-free pasta and other dishes suitable for coeliacs.

G7 ✉ Via di Ponte Quattro Capi 16 ☎ 06 686 1601 🕐 Mon–Sat 12.30–3, 7.30–11. Closed Aug 🚌 H, 23, 63, 280 to Lungotevere dei Cenci or 23, 125, 280 to Lungotevere degli Anguillara

---

RESTAURANT ETIQUETTE

Italians have a strong sense of how to behave, which applies in restaurants as much as anywhere. It is considered bad form to order only one course in more sophisticated restaurants—if that is what you want, go to a pizzeria or trattoria.

EAT

Breakfast in Rome is washed down with a cappuccino or the longer and milkier *caffè latte*. At other times espresso *(un caffè)*, a short kick-start of caffeine, or *caffè macchiato*, with a drop of milk, are the coffees of choice—Italians never drink cappuccino after lunch or dinner. Decaffeinated coffee is *caffè Hag* and iced coffee *caffè freddo*.

SUPPLIZIO €

supplizioroma.it

Supplì, deep-fried croquettes stuffed with tomato, mozzarella and rice, are a street food favorite in Rome, but here they're elevated to gourmet heights with new and classic flavors.

➕ E6 ✉ Via dei Banchi Vecchi 143 ☎ 06 8987 1920 🕐 Mon–Sat 11.30–4, 4.30–9.30 🚌 40, 46, 62, 64 and all services to Largo di Torre Argentina

LA TAZZA D'ORO €

tazzadorocoffeeshop.com

At this long-established coffee house, roasting is done on the premises and you can sample one of Rome's finest *espressi*. Stand at the old-fashioned counter or take a seat for a shot, before picking up some beans, ground coffee or specialty chocolate to take home.

➕ G5 ✉ Via degli Ormetti 5b ☎ 06 678 9792 🕐 Mon–Sat 7am–8pm, Sun 10.30–7.15 🚌 30, 70, 87, 116, 186 to Corso del Rinascimento

TORCÈ €

claudiotorce.it

Close to the Forum or the Colosseum is this fabulous *gelate-ria*, whose ices are some of the best in Rome. Flavors include eight different types of chocolate, seasonal fruits and salted peanut.

➕ H9 ✉ Viale Aventino 59 ☎ 06 9788 2939 🕐 Mon–Tue 11–9, Wed–Sun 11am–midnight 🚇 Circo Massimo 🚌 75, 118, 673

TRE SCALINI €

trescalini.it

This long-established bar and restaurant is on Piazza Navona, its tables spilling onto the square itself. It's famous for its *tartufo*, an ice cream truffle of extraordinary richness and sophistication.

➕ F5 ✉ Piazza Navona 28 ☎ 06 6880 1996 🕐 Sun–Fri 10am–midnight, Sat 10am–3am (shorter hours in winter) 🚌 30, 70, 87 and other services to Corso del Rinascimento

VECCHIA ROMA €€

ristorantevecchiaroma.com

Popularity has not spoiled this pretty, predominantly fish restaurant located at the heart of the Ghetto, with outdoor dining in summer on the picturesque piazza terrace or in the 18th-century interior.

➕ G6 ✉ Via Tribuna dei Campitelli 18 ☎ 06 686 4604 🕐 Mon, Tue, Thu–Sun 12.30–3, 8–11; closed 3 weeks in Aug 🚌 44, 46, 60 and other services to Piazza Venezia or Via del Teatro di Marcello

ZARAZÀ €

trattoriazaraza.it

If you're in Frascati, come here for tasty, traditional Roman dishes cooked with a light touch, on the terrace or in one of the attractive dining rooms.

✉ Via Regina Margherita 45, Frascati ☎ 06 942 2053 🕐 Tue–Sun 12.30–2.30, 7.30–10.30; closed Sun 7.30–10.30 Oct–May and 3 weeks in Aug

EAT

Sleep

Rome has a great range of places to stay, with options to suit all tastes and budgets. In this section, establishments are listed alphabetically.

SLEEP

Introduction

Accommodations in Rome range from opulent, traditional grandeur, through sleek modernity aimed at business travelers, to quirky boutique-style hotels, family-run bed-and-breakfasts and simple hostels for pilgrims.

Location, Location

Accommodations are scattered right across the city, with the most expensive choices along and around Via Vittorio Veneto, mid-range in other parts of the historical central core and budget places near Termini station. What to expect in terms of price and quality depends largely on location. Staying in the *centro storico* you are close to all of Rome's sights, but also to its sounds. Narrow streets and tall buildings tend to amplify the noise. Quiet places can be found, on the edge of the popular areas or in hotels with double glazing. If you value your sleep, book a room in the quieter Aventino, Celio or Prati districts. You will have to travel, but public transport is inexpensive, and hotels are often cheaper than in the heart of the city.

What You Get for Your Money

The familiar star system operates in Italy, with five stars denoting the highest standard of comfort, luxury and facilities. A one-star hotel has few facilities and may not include a private bathroom; normally the television and telephone will be in the lobby. One-star hotels tend not to accept credit cards and do not have a 24-hour desk service.

BOOKING IN ROME

Do compare prices via the various websites, but bear in mind, it is often cheaper to book direct with hotels, which may offer between 10 and 40 percent off the standard rate. Prices rise at peak season; the cheapest time to visit is January to March and August. All visitors must pay an accommodation tax of €3–€7, which is added to your bill.

From top: The pretty, ivy-covered Raphaël; entrance of the Hotel Trastevere; help with the luggage; Hotel de Russie

Directory

THE ANCIENT CITY
Mid-Range
Bolivar
Celio
Nerva
Luxury
Capo d'Africa

CENTRAL ROME
Budget
Navona
Pomezia
Smeraldo
Mid-Range
Abruzzi
Campo de' Fiori
Due Torri
La Residenza in Farnese
Luxury
Albergo Cesari
Raphaël

TRASTEVERE AND THE SOUTH
Budget
Trastevere

NORTHERN ROME
Budget
Hotel Panda
Le Petit Real
Mid-Range
Locarno
Manfredi
Piazza di Spagna
Luxury
Hassler-Villa Medici
Hotel de Russie
Regina Hotel Baglioni
Quirinale

Sleeping A–Z

PRICES

Prices are approximate and based on a double room for one night.

€€€	over €300
€€	€150–€300
€	under €150

ABRUZZI €€
hotelabruzzi.it

It's all about location at this family-run hotel, a stone's throw from the Pantheon—some rooms have views of its facade. The stylish rooms are clean-cut and simple, with huge photographic views of Rome on the white walls. It can be noisy, but it's superbly sited if you like to be in the thick of things.

⊞ F5 ✉ Piazza della Rotonda 69 ☎ 06 9784 1351 🚌 40, 46, 62, 64, 70, 81, 87 to Largo di Torre Argentina

ALBERGO CESARI €€€
9-hotel-cesari-rome.it

Welcoming travelers since 1787, the Cesari combines classic comfort with up-to-the-minute facilities. Its wonderful location in the heart of the historic center is a bonus, and the rooms are, by Roman standards, very well insulated from street noise. The service provided by the excellent staff is outstanding, and the roof garden, for breakfast or drinks, is superb.

⊞ G5 ✉ Via di Pietra 89a ☎ 06 674 9701 🚌 C3, 51, 62, 63, 80, 83, 85 to Via del Corso

BOLIVAR €€

bolivarhotel.eu

This four-star hotel is perfectly positioned for the sights of the Ancient City, in a quiet alley just off busy Via IV Novembre. The rooms are traditionally decorated, though not especially large. The breakfast room has attractive views.

➕ H6 ✉ Via della Cordonata 6, between Via IV Novembre and Via XXIV Maggio ☎ 06 679 1614 🚇 Barberini 🚌 H, 40, 60, 64, 70, 170 to Via IV Novembre or Via Nazionale

CAMPO DE' FIORI €€

hotelcampodefiori.com

Opulent textiles and rich colors are the keynotes of the comfortable rooms here. Some have balconies, and the roof terrace is a delight. There are self-catering apartments.

➕ F6 ✉ Via del Biscione 6 ☎ 06 687 4886 🚌 40, 46, 62, 64 to Corso Vittorio Emanuele II

CAPO D'AFRICA €€€

hotelcapodafrica.com

Close to the Colosseum, this designer boutique hotel boasts

The Hotel de Russie

sleek contemporary decor, with sunny, bright shades and displays of Italian modern art. You can eat dinner or have a drink on the attractive rooftop terrace.

➕ K7 ✉ Via Capo d'Africa 54 ☎ 06 772 801 🚇 Colosseo

CELIO €€

hotelcelio.com

In an enviable spot very close to the Colosseum and the Forum, this stylish hotel has an opulent vibe, with its damask wallpapers, brocaded drapes and Renaissance-style frescoes. Some rooms are definitely small, but the luxurious bathrooms make up for that, and there's a great roof terrace.

➕ J7 ✉ Via dei Santissimi Quattro 35/c ☎ 06 7049 5333 🚇 Colosseo

DUE TORRI €€

hotelduetorriroma.com

You can walk from the Due Torri to several of the city's main sights, some great shopping and a plethora of restaurants. Rooms, spread over five floors (there's an elevator), are smallish but comfortable and the public spaces are furnished with fine antiques and old prints. The fourth- and fifth-floor rooms have balconies or terraces, but this can make them much noisier.

➕ F5 ✉ Vicolo del Leonetto 23–25 ☎ 06 6880 6956 🚌 30, 70, 81, 87 to Lungotevere Marzio or Corso del Rinascimento

HASSLER-VILLA MEDICI €€€

hotelhasslerroma.com

You'll find this well-located, jet-set and VIP haunt just above the Spanish Steps and close to the Colosseum. Rooms vary considerably according to price, but all guests have access to the stunning roof terrace restaurant and garden bar.

➕ H4 ✉ Piazza Trinità dei Monti 6 ☎ 06 699 340 🚇 Spagna 🚌 117

HOTEL PANDA €–€€

hotelpanda.it

Just a few steps from classy Piazza di Spagna and the Spanish Steps, the Hotel Panda is excellent value in this pricey area. Rooms in the 19th-century palazzo may be oddly shaped in some cases, but they're clean and bright. Breakfast, not included in the price, is served in the hotel's coffee bar.

➕ G3 ✉ Via della Croce 35 ☎ 06 678 0179 🚇 Spagna

HOTEL DE RUSSIE €€€

roccofortehotels.com

A glorious hotel just off Piazza del Popolo, distinguished by its modern and stylish design. The rooms are calm and bright, and most have views of the gardens.

➕ F3 ✉ Via del Babuino 9 ☎ 06 328 881 🚇 Flaminio 🚌 117 to Piazza del Popolo

LOCARNO €€

hotellocarno.com

This hotel has genuine 1920s art nouveau decor and period furniture, with a feel of old-world elegance, along with nice touches such as an open fire in winter and a garden and delightful roof terrace. Ask for the better rooms in

the eastern annexe, not the downbeat rooms in the main building.

➕ F3 ✉ Via della Penna 22 ☎ 06 361 0841 🚇 Flaminio 🚌 C3, 301, 628 to Passeggiata di Ripetta, or 301, 628 to Lungotevere in Augusta

MANFREDI €€

hotelmanfredi.it

The creeper-clad facade of this welcoming, family-run hotel, just off Piazza di Spagna, fronts a classically comfortable and traditional type of accommodation. Rooms are sometimes on the small side, but all are beautifully furnished and equipped. The buffet breakfast should keep you going for hours.

➕ G3 ✉ Via Margutta 61 ☎ 06 320 7676 🚇 Spagna 🚌 119 to Piazza di Spagna

NAVONA €

hotelnavona.com

Rooms are well-sized at this friendly hotel, beautifully situated

SLEEP

close to Rome's finest piazza. There are good deals early every month, breakfast included, but expect to pre-pay on these. Remember that rooms facing the street are likely to be noisy at night.

🔲 F5 ✉ Via dei Sediari 8 ☎ 06 6830 1252 🚌 30, 70, 81, 87, 130, 492 to Corso del Rinascimento

NERVA €€

hotelnerva.com

In an unbeatable position for the sights of the Ancient City, the Nerva is one of only a few hotels that are within a stone's throw of the Roman Forum. Renovated modern rooms, some with original features, amiable service and a warm welcome await.

🔲 H6 ✉ Via Tor de' Conti 3–4 ☎ 06 678 1835 or 06 679 3764 🚇 Colosseo or Cavour 🚌 60, 85, 87, 175 and all other services to Via dei Fori Imperiali, Piazza Venezia or Via IV Novembre–Via Nazionale

LE PETIT REAL €

lepetitreal.it

Spacious rooms and access to excellent transportation links are the bonuses at this fourth-floor hotel near Termini. It's well-run, the staff are helpful and the breakfast is excellent.

🔲 K5 ✉ Via Cavour 58 ☎ 06 482 3566 🚇 Cavour or Termini

PIAZZA DI SPAGNA €€

hotelpiazzadispagnarome.com

The position of this good-value hotel is a major plus, just a few minutes' stroll from the Spanish Steps. Rooms vary, but all are light and airy with good bathrooms and the staff are exceptionally helpful. There's a small terrace, a real bonus in this central location.

🔲 G4 ✉ Via Mario de' Fiori 61 ☎ 06 679 6412 🚇 Spagna 🚌 117 to Piazza di Spagna

POMEZIA €

hotelpomezia.it

Near Piazza Navona and Campo de' Fiori, this modestly comfortable hotel is traditionally furnished and decorated. All rooms have private bathrooms, and there's a roof terrace and small bar. There is a specially adapted room for people with disabilities, but no elevator.

🔲 F6 ✉ Via dei Chiavari 12–15 ☎ 06 686 1371 🚌 46, 62, 64 to Corso Vittorio Emanuele II or 8, 46, 62, 64, 70, 80 to Largo di Torre Argentina

QUIRINALE €€€

hotelquirinale.it

Composers Puccini and Verdi have stayed at the charming four-star Quirinale. The high-ceilinged rooms are decorated in neoclassical style, with chandeliers, parquet

---

WHAT TO PAY

Hotels are classified by the Italian state into five categories from one star (basic) to five stars (luxury). The prices each can charge are set by law and must be displayed in the room (you will usually find them on the door). However, prices within a hotel can vary from room to room (and some hotels have off- and peak-season rates). If a room is too expensive, do not be afraid to ask for a less expensive one. Watch for extras like air-conditioning and obligatory breakfasts. Single rooms cost about two-thirds the price of doubles, and to have an extra bed in a room adds 35 percent to the bill. Note that a two-star hotel might have as much, if not more, charm than a four-star hotel.

floors, early Empire furnishings and huge bathrooms. Breakfast, which is taken in the shaded loggia overlooking the courtyard, is a delight.
➕ J4 ✉ Via Nazionale 7 ☎ 06 4707 🚇 Repubblica

RAPHAËL €€€

raphaelhotel.com

This charming, ivy-covered hotel is hidden away in the heart of the *centro storico*. There's a wide range of rooms, but the main draw is the rooftop dining terrace with views over the cityscape.
➕ F5 ✉ Largo Febo 2 ☎ 06 682 831 🚌 30, 70, 81, 87, 130 to Corso del Rinascimento

REGINA HOTEL BAGLIONI €€€

baglionihotels.com

Murano glass chandeliers, silk tapestries and marble bathrooms are some of the luxury fixtures and fittings in this Liberty-style hotel. The eighth-floor Sala Belvedere has glass walls and a sun roof with splendid views. Attention to detail and service are exemplary.
➕ H3 ✉ Via Vittorio Veneto 72 ☎ 06 421 111 🚇 Barberini

LA RESIDENZA IN FARNESE €€

residenzafarneseroma.it

This four-star hotel is located in a superb position in an ivy-hung alley and in the shadow of the great Palazzo Farnese. Originally part of a former convent, the rooms in this centuries-old building vary from former nuns' cells with small bathrooms to large, pastel-decorated salons.
➕ E6 ✉ Via del Mascherone 59 ☎ 06 6821 0980 🚌 23, 280 to Lungotevere dei Tebaldi

SMERALDO €

smeraldoroma.com

A great central location on an atmospheric backstreet not far from Campo de' Fiori and excellent value for money make this hotel a good choice. Bedrooms and public areas both have a crisp, modern look, and the rooftop terrace is a real bonus.
➕ F6 ✉ Vicolo dei Chiodaroli–Via dei Chiavari ☎ 06 687 5929 🚌 46, 62, 64 to Corso Vittorio Emanuele II or 8, 46, 62, 64, 70, 81 to Largo di Torre Argentina

TRASTEVERE €

hoteltrastevere.net

Prices vary according to room size here, but all offer good value in a central and attractive location. This hotel is popular with Italians; the bed-and-breakfast offer is a particularly good deal.
➕ E7 ✉ Via Luciano Manara 24a–25 ☎ 06 581 4713 🚌 H, 8, 780 to Piazza Sonnino or Viale di Trastevere

SLEEP

Need to Know

This section takes you through all the practical aspects of your trip to make it run more smoothly and to give you confidence before you go and while you are there.

Planning Ahead

WHEN TO GO

The best time to visit Rome is April to early June or mid-September to October, when the weather is not uncomfortably hot. Easter weekend is very busy. Many restaurants and businesses close for the entire month of August. January and February are the quietest months.

TIME

Italy is one hour ahead of GMT in winter, six hours ahead of New York and nine hours ahead of Los Angeles.

TEMPERATURE

JAN	FEB	MAR	APR	MAY	JUN	JUL	AUG	SEP	OCT	NOV	DEC
44°F	46°F	52°F	58°F	64°F	74°F	79°F	77°F	72°F	64°F	55°F	48°F
7°C	8°C	11°C	14°C	18°C	23°C	26°C	25°C	22°C	18°C	13°C	9°C

Spring (March to May) can be muggy. It can be rainy in March, and through to May.
Summer (June to August) is hot and dry, with sudden thunderstorms, especially in August. July and August are uncomfortably hot.
Autumn (September to November) is mixed but can produce crisp days with clear skies.
Winter (December to February) is short and moderately cold.

WHAT'S ON

January *La Befana* (Jan 6): Epiphany celebrations; fair and market in Piazza Navona.
February *Carnevale* (week before Lent): Costume festivities; parties on Shrove Tuesday.
March *Festa di San Giuseppe* (Mar 19): Street stalls in the Trionfale area north of the Vatican.
March/April *Good Friday* (Mar/Apr): Procession of the Cross at 9pm to the Colosseum, led by the Pope. *Easter Sunday:* The Pope addresses the assembled crowds at noon in Piazza di San Pietro.
May *Primo Maggio* (May 1): Free rock concert on Labor Day in Piazza

San Giovanni in Laterano, featuring both Italian and international artists. *International Horse Show* (early May): Concorso Ippico in Villa Borghese.
June *Festa della Repubblica* (Jun 2): Military parade along Via dei Fori Imperiali. *Lungo il Tevere* (2nd week Jun–Jul): Art, culture, music and food festival on the banks of the Tiber.
August *Ferragosto* (Aug 15): Feast of the Assumption; everything closes for at least the day.
September *Art Fair*: One of several in Via Margutta. *Sagra dell'Uva* (Sep): Wine and harvest festival in the towns of Castelli Romani.

October *Roma Europa*: International dance and drama festival October to November and beyond.
November *Ognissanti* (Nov 1–2): All Saints' Day. *Rome International Film Festival:* Various venues. *Festa di Santa Cecilia* (22 Nov): In the catacombs and church of Santa Cecilia in Trastevere.
December *Festa della Madonna Immacolata* (Dec 8): Pope and other dignitaries leave flowers at the statue of the Madonna in Piazza di Spagna. *Christmas lights all over the city*: Christmas tree and crib outside St. Peter's. *Piazza Navona Christmas Fair*: stalls, entertainment.

ROME ONLINE
060608.it
Rome's official website for tourist information has excellent practical information on the city.

adr.it
The official site of Rome's main airports, Leonardo da Vinci and Ciampino, with useful contacts and details of transportation links into the city.

w2.vatican.va and museivaticani.va
Vatican City's polished official websites offer multilingual information on the Vatican Museums, the Sistine Chapel and St. Peter's, a calendar of religious events, an online version of its official newspaper and other general information on the Vatican.

romeing.it
This excellent site covers every aspect of visiting or living in Rome. Regularly updated, it offers suggestions for eating, drinking and entertainment, as well as feature articles and help with planning your trip.

romaclick.com
This site is dedicated to accommodations deals and airport transfers, and offers a user-friendly accommodations reservation service with last-minute reductions.

romeguide.it
An Italian-based site with a wealth of daily updated information; use it for reserving museum passes and to find out what's on.

coopculture.it
You'll save yourself hours of time and skip lines by using this efficient website to book tickets ahead for entry to Rome's major museums and monuments. The site also offers information and help to plan your visits.

ristorantiroma.it
You can search this portal site using categories such as cuisine, location or facilities.

TRAVEL SITES

atac.roma.it
Rome's bus company website gives information about public transportation, including maps and how to buy the best ticket for your needs.

capitolium.org
Devoted to the Roman and Imperial forums, this site includes a wide range of historical material, including reconstructions of how the forums might have originally looked.

catacombe.roma.it
The official site of Rome's San Callisto catacombs.

fodors.com
A travel-planning site where you can research prices, book tickets, cars and rooms, and ask questions; links to other sites.

INTERNET ACCESS

Almost all hotels, and many cafés and bars, offer free WiFi. There are internet cafés all over the city, particularly in the streets around Termini. By law, you may be asked to show proof of identity in the form of your passport before you are allowed to access the internet.

NEED TO KNOW

Getting There

Check visa and passport requirements before traveling: see gov.uk or it.usembassy.gov.

EU citizens with an EHIC card are entitled to the same cover for medical treatment as Italian residents (for which they may still have to pay); insurance to cover illness and theft is still strongly advised. Visitors from outside the EU should check their insurance coverage and, if necessary, buy a supplementary policy.

TIPS

● Avoid taxi and hotel touts who will approach you at the airport. Use only licensed (white) taxis. Fares are fixed for most destinations in the city center.
● Buy your return (round-trip) train ticket online (trenitalia.com) or when you arrive at Fiumicino. The lines are much longer at Termini, and the ticket will not become valid until you stamp it on your return journey.
● You will find suitcases with wheels a godsend at Fiumicino. It is quite some distance between baggage reclaim and the exit, and for some stretches you cannot use a baggage trolley, particularly on the homeward journey.

AIRPORTS

There are direct flights into Rome from Europe and North America to Leonardo da Vinci (Fiumicino) and Ciampino airports. Visitors from Europe can also arrive by rail to Stazione Termini, or by bus to Stazione Tiburtina.

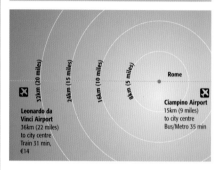

32km (20 miles)
24km (15 miles)
16km (10 miles)
8km (5 miles)

Rome

Leonardo da Vinci Airport
36km (22 miles)
to city centre
Train 31 min,
€14

Ciampino Airport
15km (9 miles)
to city centre
Bus/Metro 35 min

FROM LEONARDO DA VINCI AIRPORT

Scheduled flights arrive at this airport 36km (22 miles) southwest of the city, better known as Fiumicino (tel switchboard 06 65951). The website for both main Rome airports is adr.it. The most efficient way to reach the heart of Rome from the airport is by rail into Stazione Termini. Trains leave every 15–60 minutes (6.23am–11.23pm) at 8, 15, 23 and 38 minutes past the hour at peak times and take about 30 minutes. Catch the Leonardo Express service direct to Termini, not the service via Fara Sabina. Buses (sitbusshuttle.it) depart from Terminal 3 (8.30am–12.30am) and take up to 50 minutes to Rome's Termini and Tiburtina train stations. Taxis take from 30 minutes to two hours depending on traffic, and are expensive (€48 set fare, maximum four passengers, including luggage, to points within the Aurelian Walls). Take only licensed cabs (white) or a prepaid car with driver available from desks in Terminal 1 or Terminal 3.

FROM CIAMPINO

This smaller airport, which handles mostly low-cost and charter flights, is 15km (9 miles) southeast of the city. There are good facilities but the airport does not have a direct rail link to the heart of Rome. To get there take a 15-minute bus journey by ATRAL bus to the Metro (underground) station at Anagnina, then the 20-minute journey to Termini on Metro line A. Taxis take 30 to 40 minutes and cost around €30. Bus shuttles (terravision.eu, sitbusshuttle.it) serve various no-frills and other airlines' flights and run to Termini (from €5 one-way, €8 round-trip booked online, otherwise €6/€11 at the airport).

ARRIVING BY BUS

Most long-distance buses terminate at Tiburtina, to the northeast of the city. Although the station is some way out of the city, it is well served by the Metro (line B) to Termini or Colosseo and by local trains and numerous bus services (for example No. 492 to the center). Eurolines run buses from more than 100 European cities. For details of routes, times and tickets, visit their website (eurolines.eu).

ARRIVING BY CAR

In the days of the empire, all roads led to Rome, but in these modern times, all roads lead to the Gran Raccordo Anulare, known as the GRA. This 70km (43-mile) road encircles the city, and is always busy. From Fiumicino airport, take the Autostrada Roma Fiumicino, which leads to the GRA. If you are coming from Ciampino you will need to follow the Via Appia Nuova. From Florence or Pisa, take the A1, also known as the Autostrada del Sole. Visitors arriving from Naples should also use the A1, while those coming from Abruzzo or the Adriatic coast should follow the A24. Wherever you join the GRA, make sure you know which exit you need; your hotel can tell you which one is best.

ARRIVING BY RAIL

Most trains arrive and depart from Stazione Termini, convenient for most of central Rome. Taxis and buses leave from the station forecourt, Piazza dei Cinquecento. For train information it's best to look online; trenitalia.com has an English-language site or call 89 20 21.

DRIVING PERMIT

If you are driving and staying in central Rome, you will need a permit to drive in the city. If you are staying in a hotel, the staff can arrange this for you.

LONG-TERM PARKING

If you are arriving by car, but don't want to use it in Rome, you can leave it in the long-term parking area (Lunga Sosta) at Fiumicino airport. Long stay costs from €10 daily (from €6 if booked online at easy parking.adr.it) for 24 hours or €69 for seven days. Short-stay in "Multipiano E" costs €30 (from €19 online) daily or €5 hourly.

CAR RENTAL

All major rental firms, and some local ones, have desks at both airports and in town. Car rental is expensive in Italy and you can often get a better deal if you arrange it in advance. The minimum age for renting a car is between 21 and 25 (depending on the company), and you will need to have held a driver's license for at least a year. Most firms require a credit card as a deposit. Accident rates are high in Rome, so make sure you have adequate insurance cover. Most car rental contracts include breakdown cover.

Getting Around

VISITORS WITH DISABILITIES

Rome is not an easy place for visitors with physical disabilities. However, the Vatican City has ramps and elevators and some hotels have rooms for visitors with disabilities. Staff at airports, museums and places of interest are willing to help and taxis usually accept wheelchairs, although it is a good idea to phone ahead. Metro line B is generally accessible (apart from Circo Massimo, Colosseo and Cavour) but Metro line A and most buses are not. Transit site atac.roma.it has an English page and links with further detailed information.

Sage Traveling (☎ 888/645 7920 in US, sagetraveling.com) is an excellent English-language resource. For details (in Italian-language charts) on using both the metro and buses, go to the ATAC home page and follow the links (see Buses above). Roma per Tutti (☎ 06 5717 7094, romapertutti.it) provides information on accessibility to buildings and other facilities. In the US, also go to the Society for the Advancement of Travel and Hospitality (SATH, ☎ 212/447 7284, sath.org).

BUSES

Service is frequent and inexpensive on Rome's mostly green or red-gray regional and blue suburban buses run by ATAC/COTRAL (map ref K4, Piazza dei Cinquecento, tel 060606, atac.roma.it and cotralspa.it, Mon–Sat 8–8, Metro Termini).

The buses are often crowded and slow. Buy BIT tickets (*Biglietto Integrato a Tempo*; €1.50) before boarding, from tobacconists, shops and automatic machines displaying an ATAC sticker. Your ticket must be stamped at the rear of the bus or tram, and is valid for any number of bus rides and one Metro ride within the next 100 minutes. Roma 24 one-day (€7), Roma 48 2-day (€12.50), Roma 72 3-day (€18), Roma CIS 7-day (€24) passes and an èRoma pass (atac.roma.it) are available. Validate these the first time they are used. Services run 5.30am–11.30pm, depending on the route.

The night service consists of buses on key routes midnight–5.30am; night buses have a conductor selling tickets.

Remember to enter buses by back doors and to leave by middle doors (if you have a pass or validated ticket with unexpired time you can also use the front doors).

Buy several tickets at once as some outlets close early. There are large fines if you are caught without a ticket. Bus stops (*fermate*) list routes and bus numbers, but bear in mind that one-way streets often force buses to return along different routes, while work to extend Rome's Metro means some bus services may follow temporary diversions. Bus number 64 is especially notorious for pickpockets.

USEFUL SERVICES

● 23 Piazza del Risorgimento (for the Vatican Museums)–Trastevere–Piramide.
● 75 Termini—Forum—Colosseum—Piramide.
● 40, 64 Termini–Piazza Venezia–close to Piazza San Pietro/St. Peter's.
● Hop on and off buses to the main sights are operated by HOHO (hop-on-and-off-rome.com), Roma City Tour (roma.city-tour.com) and City Sightseeing (city-sightseeing.com).

● 81 Piazza del Risorgimento (Vatican Museums)–Piazza Venezia–Circo Massimo.
● 117 Circular minibus service in the historic center including Piazza del Popolo–Via del Corso–Via Cavour–Roman Forum–Colosseum–San Giovanni in Laterano.

SUBWAY

Rome's Metro (romametropolitane.it) has four lines, A, B, C and D. A and B intersect at Stazione Termini. Mainly a commuter service and of limited use in the city, the subway is good for trans-city rides. Station entrances are marked by a large M and each displays a map of the network. Services run 5.30am to 11.30pm (12.30am Saturday). Tickets are valid for one ride (or get a BIT, see "Buses") and can be bought from tobacconists, bars and shops displaying ATAC or COTRAL stickers, and from machines at stations—have euro coins handy.

TAXIS

Official taxis are white, with an official number and a Taxi sign on the roof. Use only these and refuse touts at Fiumicino, Termini and elsewhere. Drivers are not supposed to stop on the streets so it is difficult to hail a cab. Taxis congregate at stands, indicated by blue signs printed with Taxi. Make sure the taxi meter is reset when you start your journey (one part of the meter will display the minimum fare starting rate). Taxi ranks are available in the area at Termini, Piazza Sidney Sonnino, Pantheon, Piazza di Spagna and Piazza San Silvestro.

When calling a taxi, the company will give you a taxi code name, a number and the time it will take to get to you. The meter starts running as soon as they are called. Companies include: Samarcanda (tel 06 5551, 065551.it); and Cooperativa Radiotaxi (tel 06 3570, 3570.it). The minimum fare is valid for 3km (2 miles) or the first 9 minutes of a ride. Surcharges are levied between 10pm and 7am, all day Sunday, on national holidays, for airport trips (€48 set fare to or from Fiumicino, €30 to or from Ciampino) and for each piece of luggage larger than 35x25x50cm (13x9x19in).

NEED TO KNOW

Essential Facts

TOURIST INFORMATION

● Azienda di Promozione Turistica di Roma:
✉ Via Parigi 11 🕐 Mon–Sat 8am–7.30pm
● There are 10 information kiosks (daily 9.30–7) across the city, including:
✉ Piazza delle Cinque Lune (Piazza Navona)
✉ Via dei Fori Imperiali
✉ Lungotevere Castel Sant'Angelo–Piazza Pia
● Central number for tourist information: ☎ 060608

EMBASSIES

UK
✉ Via XX Settembre 80/A
☎ 06 4220 0001,
gov.uk
US
✉ Via Vittorio Veneto 121
☎ 06 46741,
it.usembassy.gov
Canada
✉ Via Zara 30
☎ 06 854 441,
canadainternational.gc.ca/italy
Portugal
✉ Via Guido d'Arezzo 5
☎ 06844 801, roma.embaixadaportugal.mne.pt
Spain
✉ Largo Fontanella di Borghese 19 ☎ 06 684 0401, exteriores.gob.es/embajadas/roma

BREXIT

● UK visitors should check the latest entry requirements and European Health Insurance Card (EHIC) arrangements, as a result of leaving the EU. Visit gov.uk/visit-europe-brexit.

ELECTRICITY

● Current is 220 volts AC, 50 cycles; plugs are the two-round-pin type.

MONEY

● The euro is the official currency of Italy. Banknotes come in denominations of €5, €10, €20, €50, €100 and €200, and coins in 1, 2, 5, 10, 20, 50 cents and €1 and €2.

NATIONAL HOLIDAYS

● 1 Jan (New Year's Day); 6 Jan (Epiphany; Easter Monday; 25 Apr (Liberation Day); 1 May (Labor Day); 29 Jun (St. Peter and St. Paul's Day); 15 Aug (Assumption); 1 Nov (All Saints' Day); 8 Dec (Immaculate Conception); 25 Dec (Christmas Day); 26 Dec (St. Stephen's Day).

NEWSPAPERS AND MAGAZINES

● Many Romans read the Rome-based *Il Messaggero*, and mainstream *Corriere della Sera* or the middle-left and populist *La Repubblica* (which has a special Rome edition). Sports papers (such as *Corriere dello Sport*) and weekly news magazines (such as *Panorama* and *L'Espresso*) are also popular.
● Foreign newspapers can usually be bought after 2.30pm on the day of issue from booths *(edicole)* near Termini, Piazza Colonna, Largo di Torre Argentina, Piazza Navona, Via Vittoria Veneto and several tourist sights.

OPENING HOURS

● Shops: Tue–Sat 8–1, 4–8; Mon 4–8 (with seasonal variations) or, Mon/Tue–Sat 9.30–7.30 with no lunch break. Food shops open Monday morning but may close Thursday afternoon. Some bookshops open on Sundays.
● Restaurants: daily 12.30–3, 7.30–10.30. Many close on Sunday evening and half or all of Monday. Most bars and restaurants also have

a statutory closing day *(riposo settimanale)* and many close for much of August.

● Churches: variable, but usually daily 7–12, 4.30–7. Most close on Sunday afternoon.

● Museums and galleries: vary considerably; usually close on Monday.

● Banks: Mon–Fri 8.30–1.30. Major branches may also open 3–4 and Saturday morning.

● Post offices: Mon–Fri 8.15 or 9–2; Sat 8.15 or 9–12 or 2.

POSTAL SERVICE

● Buy stamps *(francobolli)* from post offices and tobacconists.

● Post boxes are red and have two slots, one for Rome (marked *Per La Città*) and one for other destinations (marked *Per Tutte Le Altre Destinazioni)*. Newer boxes, usually blue, are for the priority mail service, or *Posta Prioritaria*.

● Vatican post can be posted only in the Vatican's blue *Poste Vaticane* post boxes. The Vatican postal service is quicker (although tariffs are the same), but stamps can be bought only at the post offices in the Vatican Museums (▷ 26–27) and in Piazza San Pietro, tel 06 6989 0400, Mon–Sat 8.30–6.30.

● The main post office (Ufficio Postale Centrale) is Piazza San Silvestro 19, tel 06 6973 7216, poste.it, Mon–Fri 8–7 (Aug Mon–Fri 8–2), Sat 8–1.15

TELEPHONES

● Telephone numbers listed in this book include the city area code (06), which must be dialed even when calling within Rome.

● Public telephones are indicated by a red or yellow sign showing a telephone dial and receiver. They are found on the street, in bars and restaurants and in *Centri Telefoni*.

● Phones usually accept phone cards *(schede telefoniche)* available from tobacconists, post offices and some bars in a variety of denominations. Break off the card's corner before use.

● To call Italy from the UK, dial 00 39 and from the US or Canada dial 011, followed by 39 (the country code for Italy), then the number, including the relevant city code.

MEDICAL TREATMENT

● Emergency rooms at: Ospedale Fatebenefratelli ✉ Isola Tiberina ☎ 06 68371, fatebenefratelli-isolatiberina.it ✉ Viale del Policlinico 155 ☎ 06 49971, policlinicoumberto1.it.

● The George Eastman Clinic (✉ Viale Regina Elena 287/b ☎ 06 7730 3258) provides an emergency dentist service. No credit cards.

● Pharmacies are usually open Mon–Sat 8.30–1, 4–8, but a rotating schedule (displayed on pharmacy doors) ensures at least one is always open. Two central pharmacies are Senato (✉ Corso del Rinascimento 48 ☎ 06 6880 3760), near Piazza Navona, and Internazionale (✉ Piazza Barberini 49 ☎ 06 487 1195), near the Spanish Steps.

EMERGENCY NUMBERS

Police, Fire and Ambulance (general SOS) ☎ 112
Police (Carabinieri) ☎ 112
Central Police ☎ 06 46861
Telephone information:
☎ 1254 (24 hours), 1254.it
International information:
☎ 1254 (8am–10.30pm)
ACI Auto Assistance (car breakdowns):
☎ 803 116, aci.it

Words and Phrases

All Italian words are pronounced as written, with each vowel and consonant sounded. Only the letter *h* is silent, but it modifies the sound of other letters. The letter *c* is hard, as in English cat, except when followed by *i* or *e*, when it becomes the soft *ch* of cello. Similarly, *g* is soft (as in the English giant) when followed by *i* or *e—giardino, gelati;* otherwise hard (as in gas)—*gatto.* Words ending in *o* are almost always masculine in gender (plural: *-i*); those ending in *a* are generally feminine (plural: *-e*). Use the polite second person *(lei)* to speak to strangers and the informal second person *(tu)* to friends or children.

BASICS	
yes	*sì*
no	*no*
maybe	*forse*
OK/alright	*va bene*
please	*per favore*
thank you	*grazie*
many thanks	*grazie mille*
you're welcome	*prego*
excuse me!	*mi scusi*
when	*quando*
now	*adesso*
why	*perchè*
who	*chi*
may I/can I	*posso*
good morning	*buon giorno*
good afternoon	*buona sera*
good evening	*buona notte*
hello/goodbye (informal)	*ciao*
hello (on the telephone)	*pronto*
I'm sorry	*mi dispiace*
left/right	*sinistra/destra*
open/closed	*aperto/chiuso*
good/bad	*buono/cattivo*
big/small	*grande/piccolo*
with/without	*con/senza*
more/less	*più/meno*
hot/cold	*caldo/freddo*
do you have?	*avete?*
exit	*uscita*
nothing	*niente*
slow	*lento*
fast	*presto/rapido*

NUMBERS	
1	*uno, una*
2	*due*
3	*tre*
4	*quattro*
5	*cinque*
6	*sei*
7	*sette*
8	*otto*
9	*nove*
10	*dieci*
20	*venti*
30	*trenta*
40	*quaranta*
50	*cinquanta*
100	*cento*
1,000	*mille*

COLORS	
black	*nero*
brown	*marrone*
pink	*rosa*
red	*rosso*
orange	*arancione*
yellow	*giallo*
green	*verde*
light blue	*celeste*
sky blue	*azzurro*
purple	*viola*
white	*bianco*
gray	*grigio*

EMERGENCIES

help!	*aiuto!*
stop, thief!	*al ladro!*
can you help me, please?	*può aiutarmi, per favore?*
call the police/ an ambulance	*chiami la polizia/un'ambulanza*
I have lost my wallet/passport	*ho perso il mio portafoglio/ il mio passaporto*
where is the police station?	*dov'è il commissariato?*
where is the hospital?	*dov'è l'ospedale?*
I don't feel well	*non mi sento bene*
first aid	*pronto soccorso*

USEFUL PHRASES

how are you? (informal)	*come sta/stai?*
I'm fine	*sto bene*
I do not understand	*non ho capito*
how much is it?	*quant'è?*
do you have a room?	*avete camere libere?*
how much per night?	*quanto costa una notte?*
with bath/shower	*con vasca/doccia*
when is breakfast served?	*a che ora è servita la colazione?*
where is the train/bus station?	*dov'è la stazione ferroviaria/degli autobus?*
excuse me (on bus, train etc)	*mi scusi*
do I have to get off here?	*devo scendere qui?*
where can I buy...?	*dove posso comprare...?*
I would like	*vorrei*
too expensive	*troppo caro*
a table for... please	*un tavolo per... per favore*
excuse me (to attract attention)	*senta*
the bill, please	*il conto, per favore*
we didn't have this	*non abbiamo avuto questo*
where are the toilets?	*dove sono i bagni?*

DAYS/MONTHS

Monday	*lunedì*
Tuesday	*martedì*
Wednesday	*mercoledì*
Thursday	*giovedì*
Friday	*venerdì*
Saturday	*sabato*
Sunday	*domenica*
January	*gennaio*
February	*febbraio*
March	*marzo*
April	*aprile*
May	*maggio*
June	*giugno*
July	*luglio*
August	*agosto*
September	*settembre*
October	*ottobre*
November	*novembre*
December	*dicembre*

TIME AND PLACE

morning	*mattina*
afternoon	*pomeriggio*
evening	*sera*
night	*notte*
today	*oggi*
tomorrow	*domani*
yesterday	*ieri*
early	*presto*
late	*tardi*
later	*più tardi*
when	*quando*
where	*dove*
Where is...?	*Dov'è...?*
Where are we?	*Dove siamo?*
here	*qui/qua*
there	*lì/là*
near	*vicino*
far	*lontano*
on the right	*a destra*
on the left	*a sinistra*

Index

We would like to thank the following photographers, companies and picture libraries for their assistance in the preparation of this book:

All images copyright AA/A Mockford & Nick Bonetti, except:

3ii AA/C Sawyer; 3iv AA/Simon McBride; 6t The Art Archive/Galleria Borghese Rome/ Collection Dagli Orti; 6ct, 6cb AA/Dario Miterdiri; 7ct Apollo & Daphne, 1622–25 (Marble), Bernini, Gian Lorenzo (1598–1680)/Galleria Borghese, Rome, Italy/Giraudon/The Bridgeman Art Library; 7cb AA/Simon McBride; 8t, 8–9ct AA/Simon McBride; 8–9b, cb, 9ct AA/C Sawyer; 9t AA/Peter Wilson; 10l Getty Images; 10r AA; 11l AA/Simon McBride; 11r epa european pressphoto agency b.v./Alamy; 14–15 AA/Simon McBride; 17tr AA/Simon McBride; 18l Dominic Jones/Alamy; 18–19 Richard Boot/Alamy; 20l AA/Jim Holmes; 20–21 Findlay/ Alamy; 21t Gone with the Wind/Alamy; 21c Scott Carruthers/Alamy; 24tl AA/Simon McBride; 24cl, 24–25 AA/Jim Holmes; 25tr, cr AA/C Sawyer; 26r AA/Simon McBride; 28–29 AA; 29tr Massimo Pizzotti/Alamy; 30, 30–31 AA/Jim Holmes; 31 Youth with a Basket of Fruit, 1594 (oil on canvas), Caravaggio Michelangelo Merisi da (1571–1610)/Galleria Borghese, Rome, Italy/ Alinari/ The Bridgeman Art Library; 32 AA/C Sawyer; 34 Erin Babnik/Alamy; 36 AA/Peter Wilson; 36–37t AA/Jim Holmes; 36–37c AA/Peter Wilson; 37tr Judith and Holofernes, 1599 (oil on canvas), Caravaggio, Michelangelo Merisi da (1571–1610)/Palazzo Barberini, Rome, Italy/ The Bridgeman Art Library; 38tl AA/Peter Wilson; 38cl, 38–39 AA/Jim Holmes; 39 Salome with the Head of St. John the Baptist (oil on canvas), Solario, Antonio da (fl.1502–14)/Galleria Doria Pamphilj, Rome, Italy/Alinari/The Bridgeman Art Library; 43cr AA/Simon McBride; 44, 44–45c, 45tr AA/C Sawyer; 44–45ct AA/Alex Kouprianoff; 45cr AA/Jim Holmes; 46–47ct AA/ Simon McBride; 47tr AA/C Sawyer; 48 Kazi Nikita/Stockimo/Alamy Stock Photo; 48–49 Rich Gold/Alamy Stock Photo; 50–51ct, 51cr AA/Jim Holmes; 54 AA/Dario Miterdiri; 54–55, 55tr AA/C Sawyer; 55cr image1/Alamy; 56 AA/Jim Holmes; 56–57 Adam Eastland Rome/Alamy; 57tr Vito Arcomano/Alamy; 57cr AA; 58tl, 58cl AA/Simon McBride; 59 AA/Alex Kouprianoff; 60–61ct Razvan Cosac/Alamy; 61br Peter Moulton/Alamy; 62 AA/Dario Miterdiri; 62–63ct AA/Alex Kouprianoff; 62–63cb, 63 AA/Jim Holmes; 66 AA/T Souter; 67bl AA/C Sawyer; 70br Adam Eastland Rome/Alamy; 71br AA/Alex Kouprianoff; 72bl AA/Jim Holmes; 73bl AA/Jim Holmes; 74bl Frank Bach/Alamy Stock Photo; 74br AA/Jim Holmes; 76br MARKA/Alamy; 77bl AA/C Sawyer; 77br AA/Simon McBride; 78 AA/Simon McBride; 80 AA/Alex Kouprianoff; 82b AA/Dario Miterdiri; 86i–ii, iv AA/A Mockford & Nick Bonetti; 86iii AA/C Sawyer; 86v AA/Alex Kouprianoff; 86vi AA/Dario Miterdiri; 88t AA/Jim Holmes; 89t AA/Dario Miterdiri; 92i AA/Jim Holmes; 92ii AA/Dario Miterdiri; 92iv AA/Alex Kouprianoff; 92v–vi AA/C Sawyer; 94b AA/Alex Kouprianoff; 98t AA/Alex Kouprianoff; 98c Ken Welsh/Alamy; 98b AA/Dario Miterdiri; 104ii–iii AA/Peter Wilson; 104vi AA/Jim Holmes; 106b AA/C Sawyer; 112t AA/Jim Holmes; 112b AA/ Peter Wilson; 116 AA/C Sawyer; 120–121ct AA/Dario Miterdiri; 120–121cb, 121cbl AA/C Sawyer; 123 AA/C Sawyer; 131ctl AA/Simon McBride; 131cb Digitalvision; 130–131b AA/ James Tims; 135 AA/Jim Holmes; 136 Digitalvision; 138 AA/C Sawyer; 140ii AA/Peter Wilson; 140iii AA/C Sawyer; 140iv AA/Terry Harris; 144 AA/C Sawyer; 148 AA/Eric Meacher; 154i–ii AA/C Sawyer; 160 AA/Peter Wilson.

Every effort has been made to trace the copyright holders, and we apologise in advance for any unintentional omissions or errors. We would be pleased to apply any corrections in a following edition of this publication.

Rome 25 Best

WRITTEN BY Tim Jepson
UPDATED BY Sally Roy
SERIES EDITOR Clare Ashton
COVER DESIGN Jessica Gonzalez
DESIGN WORK Liz Baldin
IMAGE RETOUCING AND REPRO Ian Little

ISBN 978-1-64097-329-9

SIXTEENTH EDITION

Printed and bound in China by 1010 Printing Group Limited.

10 9 8 7 6 5 4 3 2 1

A05743
Maps in this title produced from mapping © MAIRDUMONT / Falk Verlag 2018 and data available from openstreetmap.org
© under the Open Database License found at opendatacommons.org
Transport map © Communicarta Ltd, UK

Titles in the Series